CANDICE OLSON
FAMILY SPACES

PHOTOGRAPHS BY BRANDON BARRÉ

WILEY

John Wiley & Sons, Inc.

Library of Congress Control Number: 2012946047

ISBN: 978-1-118-27667-9 (pbk)
ISBN: 978-1-118-29543-4; 978-1-118-29544-1; 978-1-118-29542-7 (ebk)

Printed in the United States of America

10 9 8 7 6 5 4 3 2 1

Book production by John Wiley & Sons, Inc., Composition Services
Book design by Tai Blanche
Cover design by Susan Olinsky

Note to the Readers:

To Cory and Brandon, for proving that respect,

understanding, love, laughter, and bravery are

the essentials of being great parents . . .

And their son Xander, for making them a family.

**C**andice Olson is one of North America's leading designers and most recognized media personalities. As designer and host of *Divine Design with Candice Olson* and *Candice Tells All,* she is a favorite with viewers on W Network in Canada and HGTV in the U.S. Each week she brings a wealth of design experience and an attitude that is smart, witty, and truly unique into over 115 million North American households.

After earning her degree from the School of Interior Design at Ryerson University in Toronto, Candice launched an exciting commercial and residential design business. Considered "the one to watch" by *The New York Times,* Candice continued to receive accolades and media attention for her distinctive and exceptional work.

Candice's foray into television began when a local TV station profiled one of her award-winning design projects. Her unique approach to residential design and engaging personality led to a weekly stint as a design contributor to the show. Viewer demand for "more Candice!" led to the creation of the hit series *Divine Design with Candice Olson.* Candice and the show quickly won a huge and loyal audience and went on to achieve a milestone of over 200 episodes after eight seasons. *Divine Design with Candice Olson* continues to receive rave reviews and recognition around the world, including the more than 160 countries where the series has aired.

In 2005, Candice launched "The Candice Olson Collection," her own successful brand of licensed product lines, including upholstered furniture, fabrics, wallpaper, lighting, carpeting, case goods, and bedding. Candice's signature style is one she describes as "a fusion of traditional form, scale, and proportions with the clean, crisp, simple beauty of modern design." For more information, visit www.candiceolson.com.

The continued demand for "more Candice!" brought her to wider audiences through guest appearances on television shows such as *The Today Show, Live! with Regis and Kelly, The View,* and *The Oprah Winfrey Show.* Candice writes a bi-weekly newspaper column syndicated in over 400 newspapers across North America and is a frequent contributor to design magazines both in Canada and the U.S. For two seasons, Candice has been featured as a Celebrity Judge for the prime time hit reality show *HGTV Design Star.*

Candice spends her free time with her family, skiing in the winter and relaxing at the beach in summer. A native of Calgary, Alberta, she lives in Toronto with her husband and two children.

Table of Contents

Rooms That Multitask

2 Creative Spaces

3 Gathering Spaces

WANT TO KNOW WHERE CANDICE SHOPS?

As her fans around the world know, Candice Olson sources out the most amazing products from her favorite suppliers across North America, and now you can gain access too!

Visit **www.candiceolsonbooks.com** to find detailed information about the materials and products from all of her spectacular rooms in this book.

Happy shopping!

INTRODUCTION

n the past, family rooms were quite often thought of as simply rec (or even wreck!) rooms: that lost abyss, a dungeon-like space whose use was relegated to nothing more than pillow fights and dodge ball. Even its title, "family room," may have come from the fact that no one outside of immediate family was allowed to set foot in the space for fear they should suspect that it harbored a pack of wild hyenas! Well, being a family room today is no easy feat. As a designer, I'll admit, it's one of the most important and challenging spaces to design, because it often needs to be all things to all people of all ages and all of their interests. Whew! That's a lot of pressure on one room!

A typical family room today might have on its "to-do" list entertaining, studying, office work, hobbies and crafts, exercising, meetings or parties, viewing movies and TV, gaming (even the "old-fashioned" variety), listening to and/or making music, or preparing and serving food and beverages—the list is varied and endless. On top of the careful planning that goes into creating space for all of these functions, most of these activities come with "stuff"—very specific stuff that needs to be stored quickly and with ease.

In addition, the multi-generational, multipurpose nature of these spaces requires specific and personalized seating, furnishings, and lighting solutions. It's important that the space be sufficiently functional and comfortable to suit the needs of one or many.

Last but definitely not least, all of this planning and function have to come together in a beautiful and stylish manner that reflects the personality of the family while withstanding both the test of time and the rigors of being well used—and, if my own family is any indication, often abused!

We've just completed a large renovation of our entire home . . . and no, it isn't easier given what I do! The motivation for the entire project started with the family room—or lack thereof in the design of the old house. With our kids out of diapers and into soccer cleats and figure skates, we lacked an indoor space where our active kids could go and be active. Our new basement family room is decidedly more kid-focused right now, with high-impact drywall that can take the constant beating of hockey snapshots and skateboard runs. However, whether it's lighting, storage, flooring, or other beautiful yet practical finishes, the bones of a well-designed family room are all there. They will allow the room to grow and evolve as our family does.

I have visions of a home theater and satellite kitchen for entertaining in our future—just as soon as the danger of getting hit in the head by a flying puck subsides and my own pack of hyenas settles down a wee bit!

1 ROOMS THAT
MULTITASK

PARTY CENTRAL

CHALLENGE

Della's basement is "capital D" Dated! It is totally stuck in the 1960s, with worn, avocado-green carpet, uneven floors, chopped-up spaces, and miles of paneling. The basement nevertheless sees lots of use for family games, karaoke, air hockey, and even a little homework. But Della and her family are part of a big group of friends who do everything together, including hosting parties on a rotating basis, and Della dreads bringing them to this dark and outdated room. She'd love a chic, contemporary place that can handle everything from dancing and air-hockey tournaments to watching TV and entertaining friends.

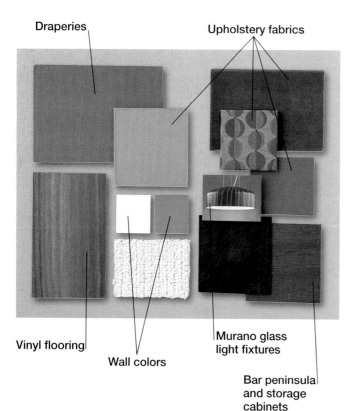

Draperies

Upholstery fabrics

Vinyl flooring

Wall colors

Murano glass
light fixtures

Bar peninsula
and storage
cabinets

BEFORE: This basement was stuck way back in the 1960s, with tons of paneling, ugly flooring and carpet, and dated furniture. It didn't matter if kids spilled grape juice on the carpet, but it certainly wasn't a room to share with anyone outside the immediate family.

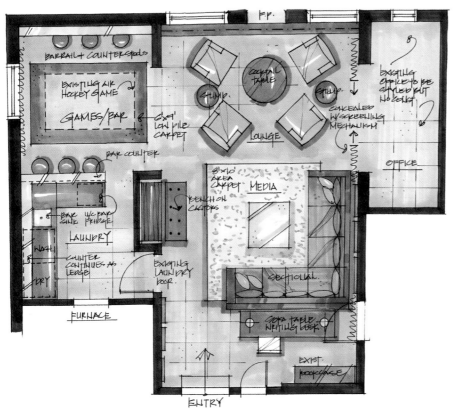

Labels on floor plan:
BAR RAIL + COUNTER STOOLS
EXISTING AIR HOCKEY GAME
GAMES/BAR
BAR COUNTER
6'x9' LOW PILE CARPET
LOUNGE
COCKTAIL TABLE
CHAIR
CHAIR
CONCEALED TV SCREENING MECHANISM
EXISTING DRAPES TO BE STYLED BUT NO SHEET
OFFICE
Fp.
BAR W/BAR FRIDGE
BAR SINK
LAUNDRY
WASH
DRY
COUNTER CONTINUES AS LEDGE!
EXISTING LAUNDRY DOOR
BENCH ON CASTORS
8'x10' AREA CARPET
MEDIA
SECTIONAL
SOFA TABLE WRITING DESK
FURNACE
ENTRY
EXIST. BOOKCASE

AFTER: Bright creamy paint and new wood-look vinyl flooring instantly update the space. A large, new sectional provides plenty of comfy seating for crowds, with another cozy conversation area centered on the fireplace.

SOLUTION

- I started by organizing this huge space into zones: An entertainment and TV zone takes up the main area; a lounge zone snuggles up to the fireplace; an office/study area gives new function to a cubicle to the right of the fireplace; and an expanded games zone takes over a small storage room to the left of the fireplace.

- To hold demolition to a minimum, I decided to keep the paneling and give it a whole new look with paint. The carpet and flooring had to go, however, and I replaced them with a wood-look vinyl flooring that's party-practical, hard-wearing, and perfect for covering uneven basement floors.

- The focal point of the new TV zone is a new, built-in big-screen TV with stereo components and speakers, but to make room for it, I had to open up the concrete-block support wall along one side of the room and install a steel beam support. Then I constructed a niche for the custom-built media center cabinetry.

- To create the new games room, I stole a little space from the adjacent laundry room and installed an elegant bar. Now the air-hockey table can move front and center, and there's storage for all of the board games too.

- The basement badly needed more lighting. I used a combination of recessed and pendant fixtures to spread light around the room and direct attention away from the stucco ceiling.

LEFT: Zoning organizes this big space according to function. The new recessed TV anchors the entertainment zone, and a former storage nook now serves as a proper games room, with the air-hockey table holding pride of place.

ABOVE: A sleek, new wood mantel gives the stone fireplace a more contemporary character, and a pair of modern lamps brings cozy light to this end of the room. A big basement needs large-scale furniture, so I chose four wing chairs upholstered in soft, pumpkin-color leather to create a lounging zone.

ABOVE: With some new furniture and track lighting, the little nook off the main area now serves as a home office and homework spot. When it's party time, the draperies can be pulled across to close off the area.

STYLE ELEMENTS

- The stone fireplace and hearth that extend across one wall had to stay, so I used the stone as the starting point for the color scheme of charcoal, taupe, pumpkin, rust, and cream.

- Before the stained paneling could be freshened with paint, it first had to be prepped with several coats of stain-blocking primer to keep the stain from bleeding through. Fortunately, the primer eliminates the need for sanding! I painted the main area with a creamy color and the games room and office area a rusty-nail hue.

- To update the lackluster fireplace, I added a sleek, contemporary wood mantel that picks up on the color of the new flooring and adds warmth and richness.

- The TV anchors a whole new seating arrangement, with two long sectionals that provide 18 linear feet of seating for big crowds. In front of the fireplace, I created a cozy spot for conversation and card games with four comfy leather wing chairs and a round coffee table. All of the furnishings are large scale to suit the size of the basement.

- Small windows are the bane of basements, so I disguised the two above the fireplace with ceiling-to-mantel draperies in a charcoal fabric.

- To screen the office from view when it's play time, I hung floor-to-ceiling charcoal-gray draperies on a metal rod that runs along the entire wall at the ceiling line. Matching panels at the other end of the room frame the sectional and hide an ugly corner door.

- Pendant fixtures illuminate the new bar in the games room, and the "granddaddy" of these fixtures hangs over the air-hockey table nearby (see page 18). These beautiful Murano glass fixtures have a clean, contemporary shape, and what I love about them is the little pumpkin-color stripe that picks up on the wall color of the games room.

BELOW: Two—count 'em, two!—9-foot-long sectionals offer Della and her family and friends loads of seating for parties and television-watching marathons. Grommet-topped charcoal panels hang from the metal rod to frame the sectional and bring some warmth and softness to the room.

OPPOSITE: Borrowing a little space from the laundry room let me enlarge a former storage nook to accommodate a beautiful new bar-height peninsula and allows plenty of room around the air-hockey table. Floor-to-ceiling drapery panels disguise a row of narrow windows that look out on what basement windows usually look out on—the grass.

LEFT: Sleek granite-look countertops give Della lots of space for fixing snacks and drinks and even serving a buffet when her crowd of friends comes over. Beautiful Murano glass pendant fixtures pick up the orange of the walls and add chic accents to the room.

FUN, FUNCTIONAL, AND KID-FABULOUS!

CHALLENGE

Jennifer has two rambunctious little boys who have taken over the whole house with their toys. With another child on the way, Jennifer wants to contain the clutter and move it all downstairs to a dedicated play space in the family's large basement. But the problem is, this space has to do triple duty, serving as a sometime guest room and a weight room where her husband can work out, as well as a rec room where the boys can let off steam.

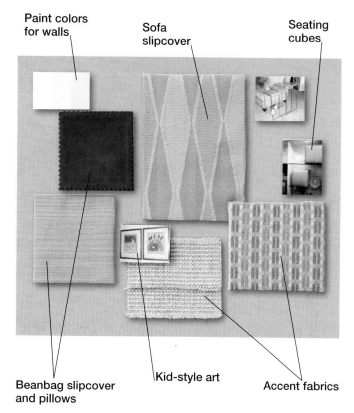

Paint colors for walls

Sofa slipcover

Seating cubes

Beanbag slipcover and pillows

Kid-style art

Accent fabrics

BEFORE: Kid clutter had taken over the whole house, including the basement, but it wasn't safe for the boys to play down here unsupervised, with Dad's free weights sitting temptingly in the corner. The sleeper sofa under the red sheet and toys accommodated guests—once it was cleared off.

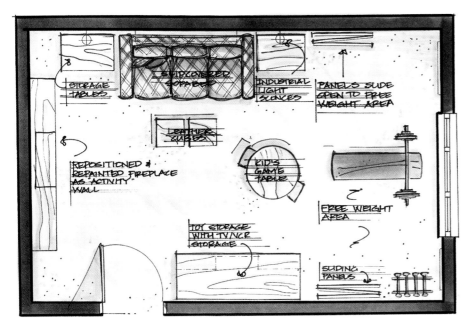

AFTER: Recognize the faux fireplace? I recycled it into an activity center and positioned it on the end wall. Durable broadloom carpet replaced the old linoleum, and a striped paint treatment livens up the walls. Folding panel doors close off the opposite end of the room to keep the weights out of bounds.

ABOVE: Panels mounted on pivots that run in a ceiling track pull back to reveal the workout area at one end of the basement (where the small windows are). When the boys are playing in the basement without supervision, the panels can be closed and locked with a childproof lock.

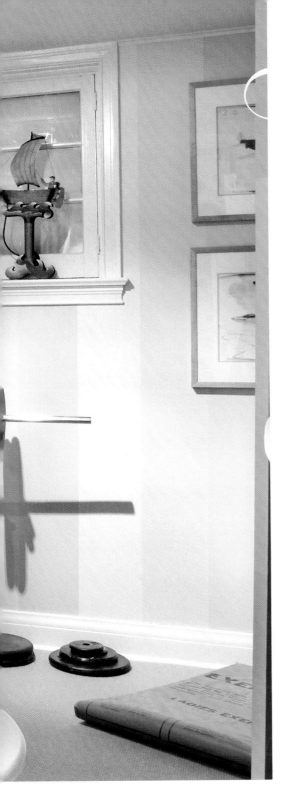

SOLUTION

- Because Jennifer and her husband want the boys to be able to play down here unsupervised, I started with the free weights, moving them to one end of the room. A clever series of pivoting panels allows Jennifer to close off this area when the boys are downstairs or when guests come.

- To organize the remaining three-quarters of the space, I moved the faux fireplace to the end wall and used it as the base for a fun new sports and activity center. New doors attached with sturdy piano hinges cover the bookshelves to provide closed storage, and a new panel fits on top, designed for pint-size basketball, hockey, beanbag toss, whatever!

- The old beige linen wallpaper peeled right off, making way for a lively new striped paint treatment that makes the ceiling seem higher.

- The beige linoleum floor tiles were ripped out and replaced with a durable broadloom sisal carpet that can take anything the boys can throw at it and will go with any look as this room grows with the family.

- In addition to upgraded track lighting, I devised some 100-percent boisterous-boy-proof sconces to frame the sleeper sofa (see page 29): Unbreakable safety-glass cylinders that fit inside cage protectors are industrial quality, kind of like something you'd see at a hockey rink! The bulbs are mirrored, so the light reflects back to the wall and causes no glare. Installing the sconces with conduit to hide the wires means there is no loose wiring to be tripped over or pulled out—and it means no drilling holes, pulling wires, and patching walls!

- To corral all of the stuffed animals and toy trucks, I hung floating shelves on the wall opposite the sofa and fitted them with bright plastic bins. Large wheeled bins slide under the unit, and the TV sits on the top shelf for easy viewing.

RIGHT: The majority of the basement is dedicated to play space for the boys. The spruced-up sleeper sofa is perfectly positioned for watching the television on the opposite wall. Paired with ottomans, it also carves out a space that can say "guest room" when the need arises.

STYLE ELEMENTS

- Paint played a key role in transforming this space, not only with graphics on the recycled fireplace-turned-activity center, but also on the walls. The basement needed a jolt of high-energy color to match all the high-energy activity going on, so I chose a tasty palette of avocado, honey, and barley for a series of 9-inch-wide stripes painted around the room. The stripes help make the ceiling seem higher, and the colors are quiet enough for a guest room yet lively enough for a kid-friendly backdrop.

- For slipcovers and pillows, I chose contract-grade fabrics. Manufactured for institutional use— as in hospitals, offices, and restaurants—they are increasingly being used in homes with kids or in high-use areas because they're so durable, stain-resistant, and long-wearing. A washable bright green and blue diamond pattern covers the sleeper sofa, and pea-green and teal slipcover a beanbag chair. (Ever tried stuffing a beanbag into a slipcover? It's not easy!)

- To provide portable extra seating and storage, I brought in a pair of upholstered cubes with lids. They also work as a coffee table and ottoman for the sofa. Now that's multitasking!

- A sturdy kid-size play table and stools provide the boys (and some friends) with a place for drawing and games. The peacock and pea-green hues match the storage bins on the floating shelves for high-energy shots of color that will be easy to change as the boys grow.

RIGHT: Even the coordinating pillows are sewn from colorful contract-grade fabrics. The super-cool sconces are virtually indestructible, made from safety glass encased in metal cages.

BELOW: Sturdy, washable, contract-grade fabric slipcovers the sofa bed. The slipcover design is ingenious—after you remove the seat and back cushions, you unzip the seat of the slipcover, and the bed folds out, so there's no need to remove the entire cover. The upholstered cubes have hinged lids that lift to reveal storage inside.

BELOW: The old faux fireplace was destined for the dumpster, but I saw a way to recycle it into this creative sports center. Striped doors cover the bookshelves on each side of the "firebox," which is now perfect for practicing slap shots. Painted panels mounted on top have cutouts for tossing beanbags and whiffle balls.

ABOVE: A custom-designed 22-inch-deep floating shelf holds the television as well as colorful bins for toys, with space below for larger bins on wheels. Theoretically, at least, it should be easy for the boys to tidy up when company comes!

CHALET INSPIRATION

CHALLENGE

The basement of Teri and Kevin's home is like a time capsule of 1960s design—a sprawling but oddly configured space with a massive brick fireplace, smoked mirrors, and barn-board trim. All that open floor space is great for tricycle races and kids' toys, but with no comfortable furniture of the adult variety, there isn't much incentive for the family to spend time together down here. The couple really want this space to be a multifunctional room the whole family can enjoy. They love skiing and sports, so I'm thinking ski lodge with a modern twist.

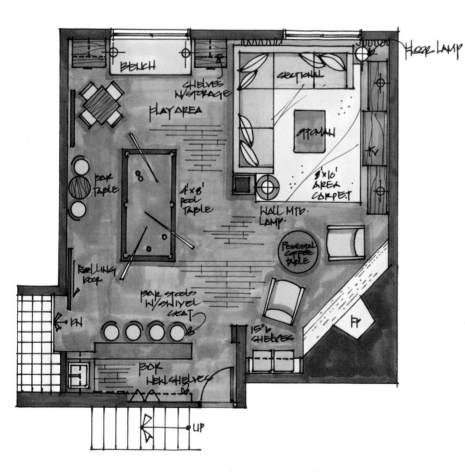

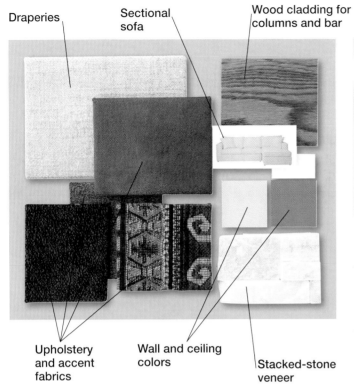

Draperies

Sectional sofa

Wood cladding for columns and bar

Upholstery and accent fabrics

Wall and ceiling colors

Stacked-stone veneer

BEFORE: A huge, open space with brick support columns and a massive brick fireplace angled across one corner, this basement was a blast from the 1960s past. It had great potential but was underutilized, serving largely as a children's play space.

AFTER: Using wood, stone, and rich, unexpected color, I created the ambience of a ski lodge without interpreting the theme literally. A vintage-look pool table and leather club chairs help set the mood too.

SOLUTION

- This basement presented two challenges: It was so big, and it was so 1960s! I started by dividing it into four zones: a kids' play zone, a bar and beverage area, a corner for games and billiards, and a television and fireplace zone for relaxing and conversation.

- The parquet floors were in good shape, so I left them in place. To tone down the overwhelming presence of brick, I covered the fireplace in a stacked-stone veneer and clad the supporting columns and bar with a modular wood system like you'd use on the floor.

- To eliminate the messiness of a wood-burning fireplace, I installed a gas insert that can be turned on with the flick of a switch.

- I ripped out the barn-board trim and painted the walls a smoky eggplant color for a rich, earthy, contemporary feeling.

- To conceal the mudroom, I installed a sliding panel on a ceiling-mounted track (see page 39).

- Behind the bar, stacked-stone veneer replaced the smoked mirrors. In addition to the wood cladding for the bar itself, I capped it off with an inexpensive but good-looking plastic laminate countertop that gives the effect of dark quartz.

LEFT: Wood flooring planks laid horizontally over the brick bar add loads of warmth and natural texture. Stacked-stone veneer brings in the feeling of a cozy mountain ski lodge.

ABOVE: Stacked-stone veneer masks the old, dark brick, and a gas insert provides warmth without the mess of wood. Leather club chairs in an updated 1930s style invite Teri and Kevin to settle in with a cup of hot chocolate—just the thing for *après-ski*!

BELOW: A new big-screen TV in a free-standing cabinet anchors the entertainment zone, defined by a comfy sectional that perfectly fits the space between the wood-clad support column and the wall. An ottoman doubles as storage and a coffee table.

STYLE ELEMENTS

- Eggplant walls might seem a surprising choice for a dark basement, but the white ceiling and light-color stone help balance it so the effect is rich and cozy. The fabrics speak to the wall color with a palette of wheat, rust, and brown.

- A big, inviting, wheat-color sectional defines the TV zone in one corner. Creamy draperies in a retro slub fabric soften the walls in this zone. To turn the short, stocky windows into a feature, I used this clever trick: I installed mirror on the wall below the windows and hung two sets of wood blinds, one over the windows and one just under the windowsill. The blinds layered over the mirror create the illusion of a full-height window whether they are open or closed.

- At the other end of the room, I flanked the windows with custom ceiling-height cabinets with cubbies for toy bins.

- The vintage pool table and a contemporary bar table and stools furnish the billiards corner with a mix of contemporary style and ski-lodge chic.

- The old globe lights were replaced with modern recessed lighting. Sconces bring more intimate lighting to the kids' zone and the TV area, and cylinder lights like you might find over a dining table illuminate the pool table in sleek, contemporary style.

- For guests, I devised a novel sleeping solution: The beanbag chair unzips and folds out to become a king-size beanbag bed!

ABOVE: The pool table anchors the "games and play" end of the room. One of the panels on the sliding track is painted with blackboard paint—good for keeping billiards scores or for kids' creativity! Wood blinds on the window match those in the TV area.

BELOW: Painted to match the wall, the track-mounted panel glides easily across the entrance to the mudroom to hide it from view. A contemporary bar table and stools give billiards players a place to wait their turn.

ARTS AND CRAFTS REVISITED

CHALLENGE

This 1920s Arts and Crafts–style home needed a good bit of TLC when Jennifer and Linda moved in with their kids and pets, but handywoman Jennifer was able to handle most of the projects. When it comes to the small, well-used living room, however, she and Linda are stumped. In addition to damaged plaster, tired bookcases, and a nondescript fireplace, the room is filled with outdated furniture that really doesn't allow the room to function well. The space needs to be all things to all members of the family while staying true to its Arts and Crafts roots.

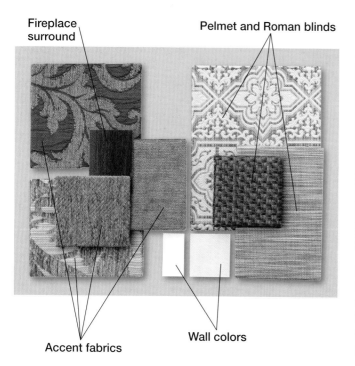

Fireplace surround

Pelmet and Roman blinds

Accent fabrics

Wall colors

BEFORE: With a hodgepodge of furniture lining the walls, this living room seemed mostly about watching TV—not at all what two professional moms had in mind for themselves and their kids. The mantel was original but seemed puny for the fireplace. And that big thing on the hearth? A whale vertebra that needed proper display!

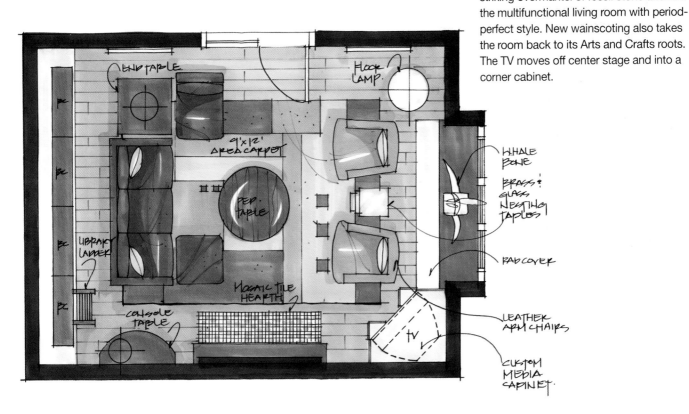

AFTER: A new wood surround with a striking overmantel of fossil stone anchors the multifunctional living room with period-perfect style. New wainscoting also takes the room back to its Arts and Crafts roots. The TV moves off center stage and into a corner cabinet.

END TABLE

FLOOR LAMP

9'x12' AREA CARPET

PED. TABLE

WHALE BONE

BRASS & GLASS NESTING TABLES

PAD COVER

LIBRARY LADDER

MOSAIC TILE HEARTH

CONSOLE TABLE

LEATHER ARM CHAIRS

TV

CUSTOM MEDIA CABINET

SOLUTION

- To take the room back to its stylistic roots, I first had to patch and repair the plaster walls and ceilings. I then covered the ceiling with embossed wallpaper to mask imperfections. To dress up the walls, I added new panel moldings that speak back to some of the detailing already in the room.

- Jennifer and Linda loved the French doors and window trim, but the mantel was puny and undistinguished. I designed a new oak fireplace surround, mantel, and overmantel in the Arts and Crafts style to visually balance the French doors on the opposite side of the room. Now it's a stunning focal point that appropriately reflects the style of the architecture.

- This room needs to be a library, a formal living room for entertaining, a casual space for watching TV, and a display space for Jennifer's whale bone—she's a biologist with an impressive bone collection and nowhere to show it off! Even in this small space, however, the zoning concept helps organize things.

- I designated the wall with the original bookcases (affixed to the wall below the ceiling) as the library space and brought in two matching bookcases from the dining room to fill the entire area above the wainscoting with continuous shelving. A really cool library ladder that glides along a metal rod gives access to even the highest shelf!

- Furniture arrangement helped refocus the room on the window and fireplace, creating a comfortable environment for conversation. Moving the TV into a vintage-look corner cabinet keeps it in range for watching, but it doesn't dominate the room. And pulling the seating away from the walls not only allows access to the library ladder but also gives the family's big dogs walk-around space!

OPPOSITE: A new sofa and ottoman make up a small-scale sectional that offers lots of seating. Behind it, a cool library ladder glides along a metal rod installed along the wainscoting, putting the vintage bookcases in easy reach. In this small space, function zones have to overlap, so the sectional does triple duty in the library, conversation, and TV-watching zones.

BELOW: In addition to new recessed lighting, I installed a ceiling fan with a period-inspired light fixture to brighten the space.

ABOVE: Classic club chairs covered in caramel-color leather complete the "conversation zone" and make a perfect frame for the "whale bone display zone."

STYLE ELEMENTS

- Arts and Crafts style is all about natural stained wood, natural motifs, and long, linear elements, especially square and rectangular shapes. The new panel molding imitates the rectangular shapes of the original wainscoting, and I incorporated the signature shapes in the detailing of the new fireplace surround and mantel as well. Instead of matching the brown stain of the French doors and window trim, I chose a darker stain for the fireplace to emphasize it as a feature in the room.

- Light creamy paint freshens the top portion of the walls, with a slightly darker tone on the paneling to call it out without too much contrast. I painted the new TV cabinet to blend in with the paneling but highlighted the antique bookcases with crisp white paint.

- For accent fabrics, I chose beautiful, warm, earthy golds and olive greens with botanical motifs that bring the outdoors in.

- To play up the window and pick up on the wood tones, I used a rust-color faux raffia fabric to cover a shaped pelmet. It mounts on the wall just under the ceiling to give the windows more height. Three Roman blinds are stitched from a fabric that alternates a lightweight, patterned weave with a strié design, giving two different effects: When the blinds are up, you see strié with a band of pattern; when the blinds are down, you see the alternating stripes.

- For furniture, I parted company with the Mission style you'd typically find in an Arts and Crafts home and went with modern comfort. A new sectional and leather club chairs are better scaled to the room than the old furniture was, and they provide as much or more seating.

- And what to do with the whale bone? I designed a new double-decker display case for it and placed it on the radiator shelf right in front of the window. Now it's a whale of a focal point for the room!

BELOW: This "everything" room even has a mini home office tucked into the corner, with space for a laptop and a letter caddy to organize bills. The little cube seat can be pulled over to the conversation grouping when needed.

SLAM DUNK!

CHALLENGE

Oliver and Mirjana have lived with their bland, boring, builder's-beige living room long enough. Furnished with mismatched furniture and kids' toys, it's the first room you see when you come in the house, and they're kind of embarrassed by the impression it makes. They're a basketball family—Oliver and Mirjana met at university, where they both played basketball, and Oliver coaches—and they would love to have a beautiful, warm, inviting space where they can entertain the entire basketball team as well as family and friends.

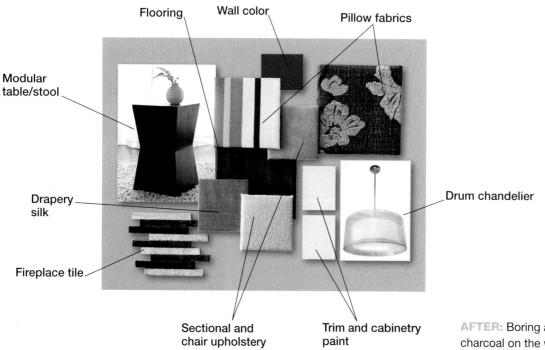

Flooring
Wall color
Pillow fabrics
Modular table/stool
Drapery silk
Drum chandelier
Fireplace tile
Sectional and chair upholstery
Trim and cabinetry paint

AFTER: Boring and bland no more! Rich charcoal on the walls and warm copper and camel hues at the windows and on the floor wrap this room in luxurious comfort. A huge sectional and a pair of armchairs solve the seating problem in style.

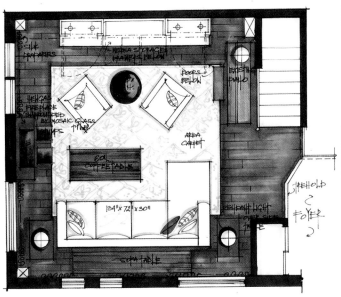

BEFORE: With beige walls and carpet and mismatched furniture, this living room didn't make the positive first impression Oliver and Mirjana would have liked. It had four big windows but no lighting, and even with the big sofa, there wasn't enough seating for the crowds the family enjoys hosting.

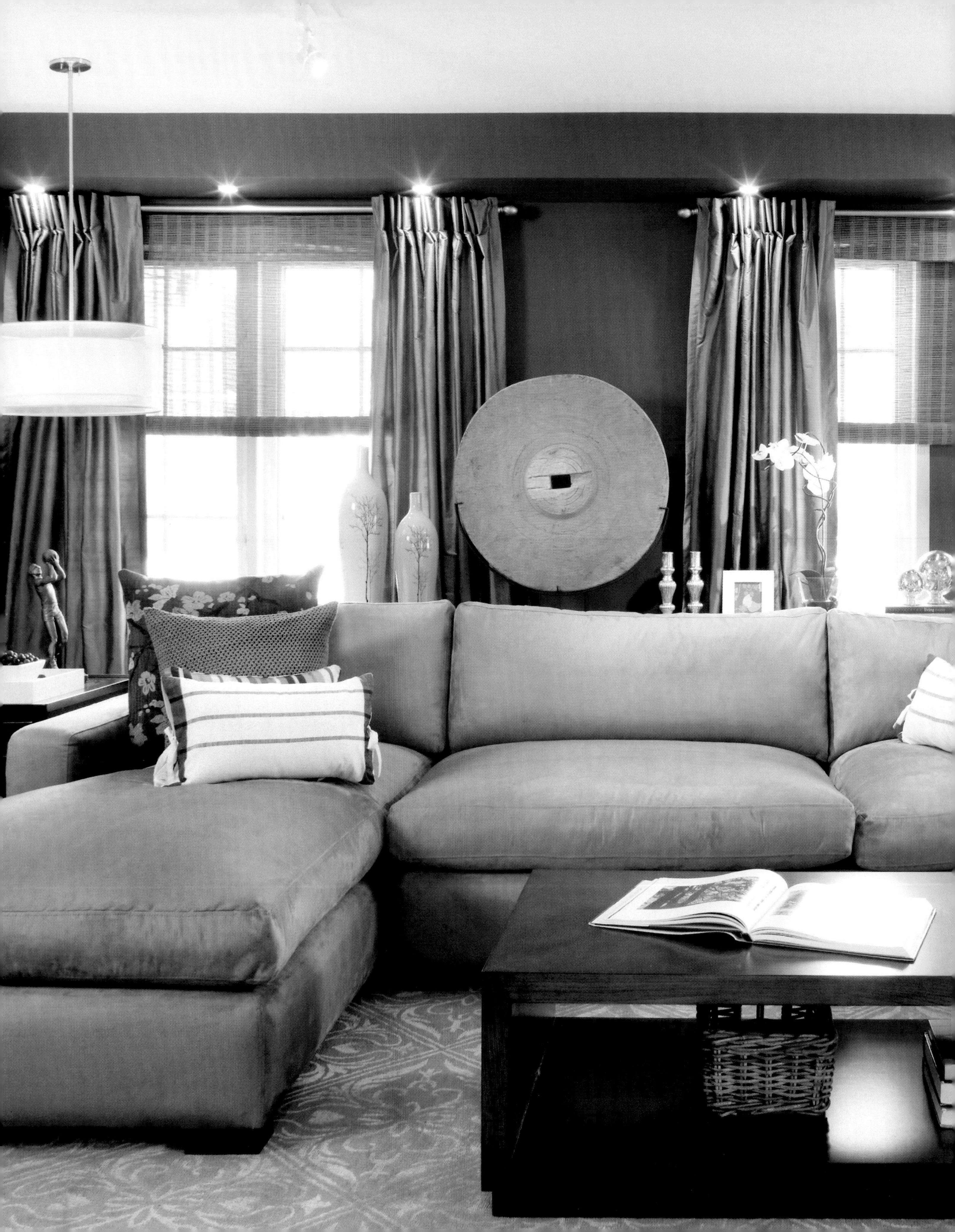

SOLUTION

- Oliver and Mirjana wanted something that says "wow," maybe even a fireplace. Fortunately, I have just the thing: a small, sleek gas fireplace insert that fits between two windows. It's an elevated, closed fireplace, so there are no safety issues for their two little children.

- To give the fireplace the necessary "wow" factor, I chose a gorgeous linear tile mosaic with the perfect combination of glass and stone tile. The tile covers the fireplace column from floor to ceiling, and the colors in the tile became the jumping-off point for the new color scheme that banishes the boring beige—dark charcoal for the walls, copper for the draperies, and smoky blue-gray for the upholstery.

- I replaced the neutral carpet with durable, easy-care hardwood flooring for a cleaner (and easier to clean), more modern look.

- The big veneer cabinetry unit got a complete makeover, with paint, additional trim, and puck lights, to make it look brand-new and custom-built.

- The piano needed to stay to remind their oldest child to practice, but the rest of the furniture (except for the cabinetry) got hauled off and replaced with all-new seating. A big sectional— and I mean big—offers 11 feet of sitting space!

- Two new lounge chairs and a 30-inch-high table allow for casual dining in here too.

OPPOSITE: Light reflecting on the shimmery silk draperies helps balance the effect of the dark walls. Easy-care microfiber is the perfect kid-friendly, crowd-friendly upholstery fabric for the sectional. Its clean lines and plump cushions combine modern simplicity with everyday comfort.

LEFT: A drum pendant suspended over the side table leaves the table surface free for snacks. Funky floral pillows pull out earthy colors in the fireplace tile.

STYLE ELEMENTS

- Comfortable seating for a crowd is key in this living room. A long, L-shaped sofa covered in durable, easy-to-clean blue-gray microfiber is perfect for kids, family, and a basketball team.

- For the pair of lounge chairs that frames the conversational grouping, I chose a really soft fabric with a great "hand" in the creamy tones found in the tile.

- Beautiful, shimmery copper silk draperies frame the windows. I kept the heading simple and contemporary to harmonize with the clean lines of the furniture and added woven blinds for texture and light control.

- The old veneered cabinetry had to be sanded first to cut the glossy finish. Then I painted it a soft, creamy, natural wicker color, added trim to extend it to the bulkhead, and backed the shelves with mirror. Interior lighting provided the final touch to give it the look of high-end custom cabinetry.

- Recessed lights around the room's perimeter highlight the cabinetry and fireplace, and puck lights in the bulkhead over the long wall of windows shine down on the draperies and make them glow. To keep the side tables free for snacks and drinks, I framed the sectional with a pair of drum pendants with organza shades.

RIGHT: Now this is what I call "wow" factor! Incredibly beautiful glass and stone tile in a linear cut frames a small, contemporary fireplace that creates visual as well as physical warmth. Wooden stools in front of the fireplace can do double duty as extra seating or side tables.

ABOVE: Creamy wicker-color paint revives the old veneer cabinetry. A solid panel behind the television helps unify the once-open shelves into a single unit. Puck lights and new glass shelves with mirror backing give the piece a fresh, contemporary look, and an extra row of cubbies fills the space to the bulkhead so the piece looks built-in.

CONCEALED AND CAMOUFLAGED

CHALLENGE

Kimberly, a professional photographer, and her family travel to exotic places for her work, but they only have to go down to their basement to travel back in time! They've been painstakingly renovating their 1970s house in a sophisticated, contemporary style but aren't sure what to do with the downstairs space. With its bright-orange swirled stucco walls, sage-green wainscoting and beams, ugly fluorescent lights, and massive brick fireplace, the room is stuck in a disco time warp. Kimberly and her husband, Jay, need the space to serve several purposes: guest room, storage space, and place to relax and watch TV.

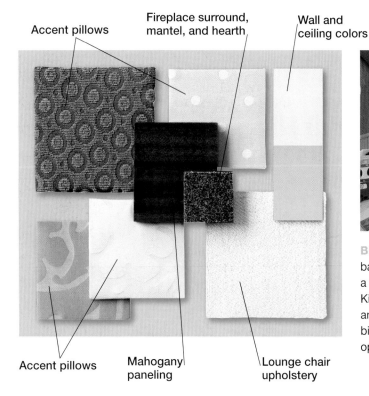

Accent pillows

Fireplace surround, mantel, and hearth

Wall and ceiling colors

Accent pillows

Mahogany paneling

Lounge chair upholstery

BEFORE: The 1970s called, and they want their basement back! Garish orange walls with a swirled stucco finish and a massive brick fireplace were outdated and unlovely, and Kimberly and Jay had turned over the space to kids' toys and random storage. When they watched TV, they needed binoculars, since the television was in an armoire at the opposite end of the room from the sofa.

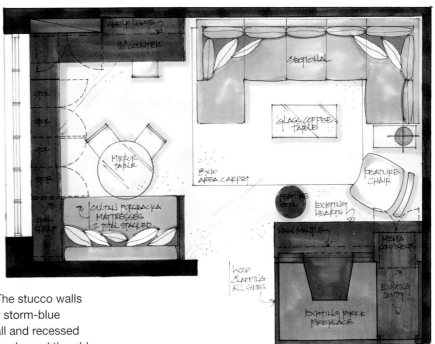

AFTER: What a difference color can make! The stucco walls and wainscoting are still there, but unified by storm-blue paint, they're no longer objectionable. Drywall and recessed lights replaced the beams and fluorescent panels, and the old brick fireplace is now swathed in gorgeous mahogany for a sophisticated, upscale look.

ABOVE: The totally reworked fireplace is now a fabulous
focal point for the entertainment/lounge area of the basement.
A storage-rich cabinet covers the brick wall and the old
open cubicle that held firewood. A faux stucco product that
resembles granite makes an economical, heat-proof surround,
hearth, and mantel for the fireplace.

SOLUTION

- I knocked off the old ceiling beams and took out the fluorescent fixtures, then covered the ceiling with drywall.

- Instead of tearing out the fireplace and starting over, I completely concealed the dated brick by cladding it in mahogany panels. This required attaching 2x4s to the brick at regular intervals, almost like wall studs, and then securing the hearth-to-ceiling panels with a 23-gauge nailer, so the paneling looks smooth and seamless.

- I covered the old firewood-storage area with a beautiful new ceiling-height cabinet to store all kinds of media equipment and accessories.

- For the new mantel and fireplace surround, I used a really cool exterior product that looks like granite but is much more economical and is completely heat-proof. It also covers the old hearth.

- Kimberly and Jay need lots of storage down here to hold the kids' toys, so I put in an entire wall of mahogany cabinets under the high windows (see pages 58–59). A daybed and an office area carve out a comfortable place for guests as well as a handy little home office/homework corner.

- With all the gorgeous wood claiming a big chunk of the budget, I decided to keep the stucco walls and wainscoting and disguise them with paint. Using the same color on the wainscoting, chair rail, walls, and bulkhead unites the hodgepodge of finishes.

RIGHT: A cushy sectional defines a cozy lounge area opposite the fireplace and television—which Kimberly and Jay can now see easily, without the use of binoculars! A glass-and-chrome coffee table adds a functional surface for snacks and drinks without taking up space visually.

The chaise portion of the sectional acts as a little room divider, separating the entertainment/lounge area from the guest room/storage end of the room. The beige carpet was in good condition (newer than the rest of the basement's décor!), so I left it in place and layered a beautiful contemporary area rug over it to anchor the seating group.

STYLE ELEMENTS

- After priming the stucco, I covered the walls, top to bottom, with a beautiful, moody storm-blue.

- A large, U-shaped sectional in a tone that matches the wall color provides a ton of comfortable seating for the family. Keeping the wall and sectional colors similar creates a smooth transition from furniture to background and helps enlarge the sense of space.

- A modern lounge chair upholstered in a creamy, kid-friendly fabric sits by the fireplace to provide extra seating for guests.

- For the daybed, I covered two twin mattresses with fitted, zippered slipcovers that speak back to the sectional upholstery. They're stacked on a wood platform, so when guests need to bunk down, they simply put one mattress on the floor, whip off the slipcovers, and put on the sheets.

- Loads of pillows in kid-proof microfiber fabrics add comfort and depth to the daybed and accent the sectional too. In addition to the usual 16-inch-square pillows, I made up three 18-inch squares in a sophisticated gray damask and three big 24 x 11-inch lumbar pillows in a washable cream to provide plenty of cushions to lean against.

- Lighting is key to adding warmth in this basement. To create layers of light, I installed recessed overhead fixtures as well as clean, traditional sconces for more intimate lighting.

- Kimberly's photography is on display throughout the house, so to bring it down here and make it a focal-point feature, I used a really cool new photo-display technology. I had some of Kimberly's black-and-white photos enlarged and printed on transparent film, which is then dropped into frames that mount over light fixtures on the wall. The backlit photos glow with life and look spectacular! Best of all, Kimberly can change the photos as she takes new ones.

OPPOSITE: The window-height cabinets hide children's toys and games. With a petite pedestal table and some contemporary chairs, this end of the room doubles as another lounging area or a spot for games. The long desk against the wall gives Kimberly space for a home office.

ABOVE: Illuminated by a pair of sconces, the daybed anchors the guest room end of the basement. When company comes, the twin mattresses can be unstacked, their slipcovers zipped off, and sheets and blankets tucked in place.

BELOW: A super-cool backlit photo display system showcases some of Kimberly's photos above the sectional. The enlarged photos are printed on transparent film, which is fitted into frames that mount over light installations on the wall.

ABOVE: An Eames-style chair upholstered in easy-care fabric swivels on its pedestal to face the sectional for conversation or toward the fireplace for watching TV. A ceiling-height mirror helps bounce light back into the room.

FROM CHAOS TO CLUTTER-FREE

CHALLENGE

Philip and Linda have one incredibly busy family. He is a police officer who also directs a downhill ski club for underprivileged kids. She is an artist who also writes computer programs for embroidery and volunteers with senior citizens. Their two kids are sports nuts who share a paper-delivery route. All of their many activities converge in the basement, which has become a dumping ground for the piles of paraphernalia that come with sports, multiple jobs, and volunteer activities, as well as a refuge for outdated furniture. The family would love to have this room be a casual, stylish space that functions efficiently for all of them—and that welcomes overnight guests as well.

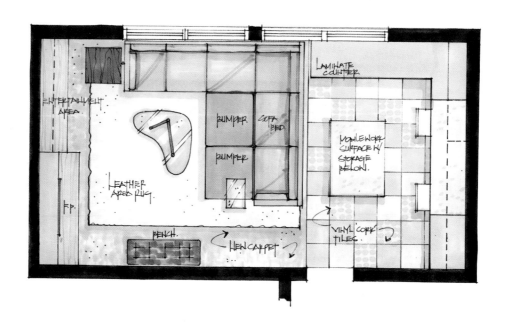

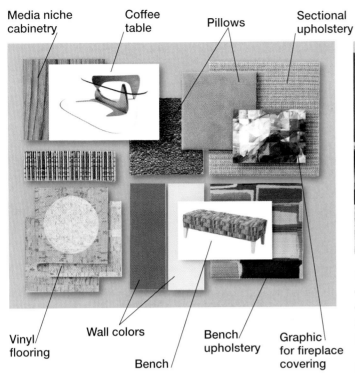

Media niche cabinetry

Coffee table

Pillows

Sectional upholstery

Vinyl flooring

Wall colors

Bench

Bench upholstery

Graphic for fireplace covering

BEFORE: Furniture from the 1960s, 1970s, and 1980s congregated here without much thought or planning. Old carpet, a messy wood-burning fireplace with an ugly brick surround, and an acoustical-tile ceiling only contributed to the unappealing environment of chaotic clutter.

AFTER: Order reigns supreme now that the basement has been zoned for function: a work and storage zone for the kids and Linda and a beautiful new lounging area for Philip (and the whole family) that includes a sleeper sofa for guests.

SOLUTION

- The basement needs to be a super-functional, super-organized space where the kids can sort and roll newspapers, Linda can store art supplies and work on her art and computer programs, and the whole family can watch TV. I started by moving all of the sports gear out into the hall and organizing it with a wall-hung storage system. Then I ripped out the old carpeting, paneling, ceiling tiles, and cabinetry to start with a clean slate.

- I divided the rec room into zones to meet all of the different needs. The fireplace was the logical anchor for a new lounging zone with a big sectional, so I dedicated the other end of the room to work and storage.

- A long, continuous L-shape counter with cabinets above and storage, storage, storage below organizes the clutter (ahem, creative materials) that Linda uses to make art. A new island is ideal for the kids to prep newspapers for delivery as well as for Linda's framing projects.

- In the work and storage zone, I laid down a budget-friendly, hard-wearing floor of vinyl tiles that look like cork. For the lounging and guest-bed area, I installed a neutral-color nylon solution-dyed carpet that's easy to clean and stain-resistant.

- I replaced the old wood-burning fireplace with a new high-efficiency gas insert and drywalled over the outdated brick in preparation for a spectacular new treatment: a vinyl paper printed with a greatly enlarged, digitally mastered version of one of Linda's favorite paintings.

- The wall beside the fireplace was the perfect spot for the new media center, with floating shelves and a new large-screen television. The cabinetry that supports the television takes advantage of an existing knee wall for sturdy support.

LEFT: To break up the long expanse of countertop, I used two laminate finishes. The oak color speaks to the cabinetry at the other end of the room, and the yellow picks up on the wall color. We needed a lot of cabinetry, so I used MDF (medium-density fiberboard) to keep the cost down and painted it to match the walls.

ABOVE: Tons of new open and closed storage organize Linda's art supplies, and miles of lovely countertop (including the island) give the kids plenty of room to assemble and roll newspapers for delivery. The waist-high work island is also perfect for framing paintings.

ABOVE: One of Linda's paintings, enlarged and printed on vinyl, makes a spectacular new finish for the old brick fireplace and inspires the wall and fabric colors. Puck lights installed in the media cabinetry enhance the illusion that the shelves are floating.

STYLE ELEMENTS

- Linda's painting was the jumping-off point for the room's design concept. Besides supersizing it to clad the fireplace, I used it to guide the color palette: a soft golden wheat for walls and storage cabinets and a spicy red for the accent wall in the media niche.

- The painting also inspired the fabrics—a wheat-color strié for the sectional, burnt orange and sage for pillows, and a geometric for the bench cover.

- The countertops in the work area needed to be super-hardworking and durable. I chose two laminates, one an oak color to pick up on the media-niche cabinetry across the room and the other a yellow that blends with the wall color.

- A comfortable, versatile sectional defines the lounging area. One section pulls out to make a bed for guests, and two upholstered bumpers turn any comfy seat into a chaise (see pages 68–69).

- The wall opposite the sectional is perfect for a gallery to showcase some of Linda's paintings.

- To cover the long, skinny windows that run the length of the room, I hung woven wood blinds. When they're lowered all the way, they hang well below the window frames to give the illusion of bigger windows. Another great feature: They can be raised to the top of the window or lowered to the bottom to let in a little more light (see page 70).

- Even with the windows, the basement needed lots of recessed lights in the ceiling to illuminate the space. Halogen strip lights under the cabinets in the work area shed bright light on the countertops, and a pendant fixture drops down at one end of the sectional to bring more light into the room.

RIGHT: One long wall becomes a gallery to display Linda's paintings. A bench upholstered in a painting-inspired geometric print provides extra seating when friends come over.

LEFT: Upholstered bumpers, those big square ottomans snuggled up to the sectional, turn cozy seating into lounge chairs. An iconic modern coffee table brings in sophisticated style and family-friendly function. To anchor the seating area, I layered a neutral-color area rug over the new nylon carpet. The toasty color and touchable texture add inviting warmth to this "relax and play" end of the room.

OPPOSITE: A cool, contemporary pendant fixture with a pierced shade hangs over the end table to bring accent lighting down into the room. The woven wood blinds can be lowered from the top (as they are here) or raised up under the matching valance.

BELOW: I turned the super-wide hallway leading to the basement into a storage area for all the sports gear. The same vinyl tile I used in the work-and-storage zone of the rec room continues out into the hall.

DRESSED UP AND FAMILY FRIENDLY

CHALLENGE

Jeannine and Patrick's basement has lovely parquet floors and a stunning carved stone fireplace that would be right at home in a formal living room—or maybe a castle! In this casual family room, however, the off-center fireplace is too elegant for the room, and the furniture is too casual for the fireplace. The couple's two boys have lots of books and toys that Jeannine would like to have stashed out of sight, and Patrick would like the space to serve as a home theater as well as a place to relax. My challenge is to turn this no-style, no-storage, no-personality room into a functional, comfortable gathering space where the family can entertain, play, and watch TV.

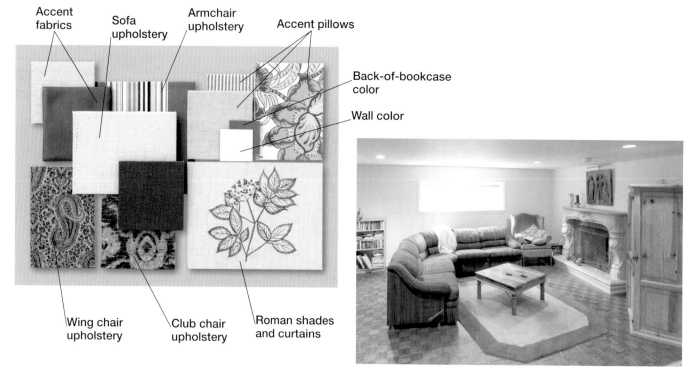

BEFORE: A beautiful carved stone fireplace seemed the natural focal point of this large, open basement, but it was too formal and elegant for the casual, family-friendly mood that the couple wanted.

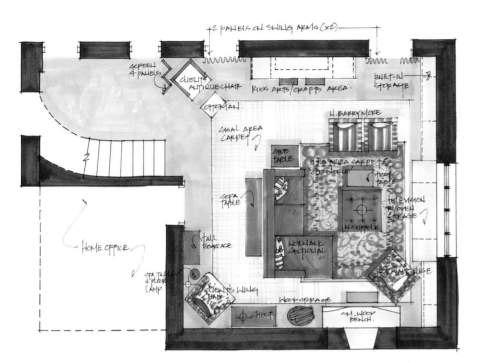

AFTER: Shifting the focus to the window and beefing it up with wall-to-wall built-in storage offsets the fireplace without ignoring it entirely. New furniture is more refined than the old oversized sectional sofa but still comfortable and welcoming.

SOLUTION

- Completely reconfiguring the furniture arrangement shifts attention from the fireplace to the window, helping downplay the impact of the ornate stone surround. The window is long and narrow, but I make it a strong feature with lots of new, built-in functional cabinetry around it. The new arrangement takes the heat off of the original focal point, the fireplace, and still allows everyone in the seating group to enjoy both the fireplace and the TV.

- The "great wall of cabinetry" not only solves all of Jeannine and Patrick's storage woes but also contains the family's large flat-screen TV. The cabinetry solves another problem too. The old furniture arrangement left the window high and dry on the wall and emphasized the fact that this was a basement. With the top of the media center cabinet reaching the windowsill, the window feels lower, anchored to the furniture, and the room doesn't seem so subterranean.

- The boys have a rough-and-tumble play space upstairs, so the family room needs to include only an area for quiet play. A long table with leaves that fold both up and down provides an activity area that can expand as needed for games and projects. A bulletin board on either side of the table gives each child a spot to personalize with photos and other neat stuff.

- I got rid of the bulky, threadbare sectional sofa and the too-country pine entertainment center and brought in new furnishings that balance elegance with casual comfort.

- Lighting is an easy way to add elegance to a room. I installed a pair of semi-traditional sconces over the fireplace to bring it into better scale with the low ceiling. Over the main conversation area, I hung a lantern-style pendant fixture. Recessed lights around the perimeter provide overall lighting to banish the basement blues, and picture lights over the bulletin boards provide bright accents.

ABOVE: An entire wall of cabinetry (built in sections and installed on-site) frames the window and solves all of the family's storage problems. Mounting the Roman shade a few inches from the ceiling makes the long, narrow window seem taller.

ABOVE: A big, kid-friendly leather ottoman and a pair of tailored armchairs help anchor the new gathering space in front of the TV.

STYLE ELEMENTS

- Fabrics are key to the casual, elegant mix that Jeannine and Patrick wanted. I started with a traditional floral that provides the cue for all of the colors in the scheme—wheat, chocolate, raspberry, and green. The floral appears on accessories around the room and helps tie all of the individual elements together.

- For the new sectional sofa, I chose a warm, wheat-color fabric that looks like linen but is actually a hard-wearing woven fabric that speaks back to the floral. A pair of armchairs wears a tailored chocolate-and-raspberry stripe, and a cozy club chair beside the fireplace is upholstered in a beautiful chenille damask.

- For graphic punch, I pulled the chocolate-raspberry color out of the fabrics and painted it on the backs of the open cabinets.

- Linen-color paint on the walls makes the perfect light-reflecting, space-expanding backdrop for the fabrics and furnishings.

- To improve the dimensions of the window, I hung an easy, breezy Roman shade 6 inches above the top of the window frame. The fabric, a simple wheat-color linen with paprika-hued embroidery, picks up on both the sofa color and the painted backs of the cabinets and adds a touch of elegance.

- I used the same fabric for panels hung over two of the room's numerous doors. The curtains soften the walls and add a sense of dramatic entry (it's dramatic, even if the entry is into a storage closet!).

RIGHT: A pair of sconces brings the ornate fireplace into scale with the low ceiling. Along with the lantern-style pendant over the seating area, the sconces help balance the elegance of the carved stone.

BELOW: The new sectional sofa is comfortable and informal but more tailored and in better scale with the room than the old threadbare sectional. Accent pillows covered in the key floral print contain all of the important colors in the room's scheme.

ABOVE: An antique chest and mirror anchor a secondary seating area along the fireplace wall. New upholstery revives the couple's old wing chair, and a pair of suede-covered drums double as movable tables and storage.

ABOVE: The boys have a rough-and-tumble play area upstairs, so I designated one wall in the family room as a quiet play area. The activity table has a leaf that can fold down to make a larger surface for games or projects. Twin bulletin boards give each boy a place for photos and notes, with picture lights shining down for illumination. Curtains hide two of the room's many doors and add softness and warmth to the space.

BELOW: Jeannine and Patrick bought this carved chair from the previous homeowners, and when they inspected it more closely, they discovered that it came from Jeannine's great-uncle's furniture factory! I spruced it up with new upholstery on the seat and highlighted it with an upholstered folding screen and uplight.

2 CREATIVE SPACES

CRAFTERS' HEAVEN

CHALLENGE

Hazel and Jude are one multitalented couple. Hazel sews, does crafts, and works full-time outside the home. Jude, a stay-at-home dad, can build anything, plus do wiring and plumbing. Together they have almost single-handedly renovated the big, old house they share with their twin 10-year-olds. There are still lots of details to wrap up, so although the family's unfinished basement would be perfect for a much-needed family room with space for crafting and sewing, Hazel is reluctant to add anything else to Jude's to-do list. They asked me to tackle the basement while Jude focuses on tidying up the loose ends in the rest of the house.

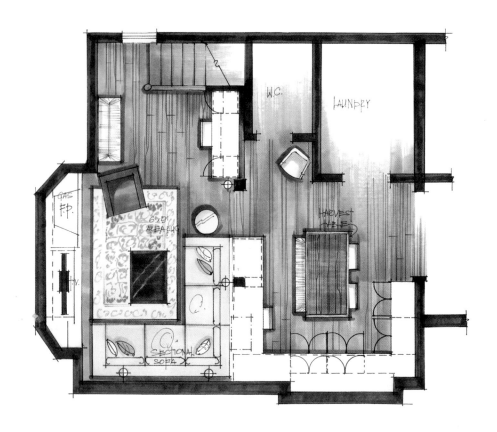

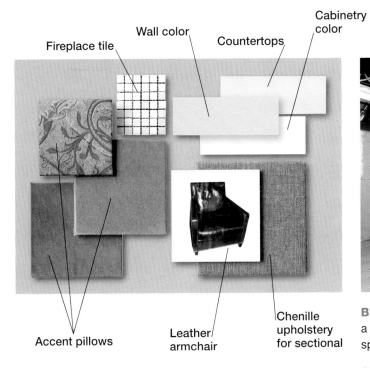

Fireplace tile

Wall color

Countertops

Cabinetry color

Accent pillows

Leather armchair

Chenille upholstery for sectional

BEFORE: With insulation packed between the wall studs and a poured-concrete floor, this basement was one big, unfinished space just waiting for attention.

AFTER: Traditional cabinetry and crown moldings and cherry-toned engineered-wood flooring bring the style upstairs down to the gorgeous new family room. Cabinetry divides the space into a TV/lounging area and a super-organized sewing and crafting zone.

SOLUTION

- The first order of business was to install walls, ceiling, and floors! I then used the support column and center beam to define the dividing line between two zones, one for all of Hazel's sewing and crafting activities and the other for relaxing and watching TV.

- For the arts and crafts area, I designed a U-shaped space and filled it with gorgeous, floor-to-ceiling custom cabinetry—and lots of it. Drawers, shelves, and open cubbies hold all of Hazel's supplies—fabric, thread, and materials for beading, card-making, and crafting. I designed a pass-through on one side of the U to allow a view from the arts and crafts area to the TV.

- In the lounge area, a fabulous feature wall of cabinetry anchors the space and showcases a big flat-screen TV and an elevated gas-insert fireplace.

- At the foot of the stairs, more built-in cabinetry provides a roomy desk area with closed and open storage. Throughout the basement, each type of cabinetry is functional and hardworking, geared to the type of activity in that area.

LEFT: Wood-and-rush chairs and a bench bring a touch of rustic European style to Hazel's crafts area. Burnished bronze pendants with vintage-inspired glass shades reinforce the traditional look of the cabinetry.

ABOVE: Loads of beautiful white cabinetry help brighten the windowless basement. I also installed recessed lights in the ceiling around the perimeter of each activity zone and used sconces and pendants to provide targeted task and ambient lighting.

ABOVE: With a clear view of the television and fireplace, the work table is ideally positioned for folding laundry or working on crafts projects. Cherry-toned engineered-wood flooring unifies the spaces with rich warmth.

STYLE ELEMENTS

- Hazel and Jude wanted the new family room to reflect the same traditional style they have upstairs, so I continued the crown moldings and cherry-toned wood flooring found elsewhere in the house.

- The traditional style of the kitchen cabinetry comes downstairs too. Bright-white recessed-panel cabinetry washed with an antique glaze unifies the entire space and looks like it's been there forever. I even encased the metal support columns in wood to create classic square columns framing the opening between the arts and crafts area and the lounge area.

- For a rich, durable work surface in the crafts area and on the homework desk, I chose the perfect countertop: a sand-speckled quartz. The light color and quiet pattern blend seamlessly with the cabinetry, and the smooth quartz surface is ideal for beading and crafting.

- An old wood-and-iron work table and a couple of ladder-back, rush-seat chairs bring a rustic touch to the arts and crafts zone. The table is perfect for laying out fabric, doing crafts, or folding laundry. Vintage-look burnished bronze pendants illuminate the crafts table and reinforce the traditional style.

- The gas-insert fireplace needed a noncombustible material for the 8-inch-wide surround, and I chose a white tile mosaic to blend with the cabinetry. I have to admit that I was surprised to discover when it arrived that it had toffee-colored tiles randomly scattered among the luminous white ones. Fortunately, the color worked beautifully with the caramel-color accent pillows!

- To give the family lots of room for lounging and watching TV, I brought in a beautiful 10 x 10-foot sectional sofa upholstered in soft, buttery gold chenille. A dark leather lounge chair complements the sectional and rounds out the seating group.

- To complement the warm-color fabrics and creamy cabinetry, I chose a soothing, cool tone for the walls: a grayed robin's-egg blue.

- Hazel loves botanical prints, so I filled one entire wall with some of her favorites hung picture-gallery style.

- The basement has no natural illumination, so I installed recessed fixtures around the perimeter of both areas to wash the walls and cabinetry with light. Traditional-style sconces also help brighten the lounge and study areas.

BELOW: Hazel's sewing machine sits in the pass-through so she can watch TV while she sews. In the open cubicle above, her mother's antique sewing machine enjoys a special place of honor.

Because all of the cabinetry is traditional, I mixed things up a bit with a modern sectional. Yummy accent pillows in pumpkin, peacock blue, and soft gray-blue contrast with the expanse of solid color. A tightly spaced grouping of botanical prints creates a focal point on the end wall.

ABOVE: A few dark accents—a rich, dark brown leather armchair, a black side table, and a black coffee table—anchor the light, airy color scheme. The area rug brings the gold, cream, and blue palette to floor level in a low-contrast pattern that plays against the expanse of solid upholstery on the sectional.

BELOW: A built-in desk with lots of storage for school supplies tucks into the space beside the stairs. Under-cabinet light strips illuminate the surface for reading and computer work. Sorry, kids, but this means no excuses for not doing your homework!

A NIGHT AT THE MOVIES

CHALLENGE

Pamela's underutilized basement is basically a catchall for odds and ends of furniture and accessories, with a corner for a not-very-inviting home office. With two of her three daughters away at university, the house was something of an empty nest. Now the girls are moving back home, and the three sisters have persuaded their mom to turn the basement into a hip new space for watching movies and practicing dance moves—one of the girls loves hip-hop. Pamela is open to the idea but wants to make sure it's a multifunctional space everyone can use and enjoy.

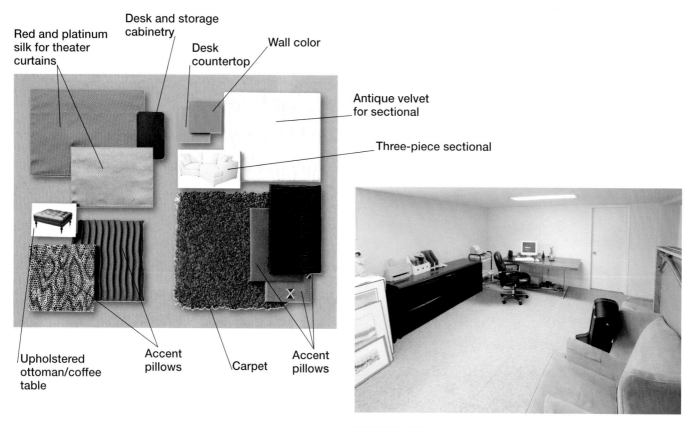

Red and platinum silk for theater curtains

Desk and storage cabinetry

Desk countertop

Wall color

Antique velvet for sectional

Three-piece sectional

Upholstered ottoman/coffee table

Accent pillows

Carpet

Accent pillows

BEFORE: With white walls, beige carpet, and fluorescent lighting, the basement was a very tidy storeroom for castoff furniture and stacks of framed artwork the family no longer used. A home office occupied one corner, but it wasn't a space anyone wanted to spend much time in.

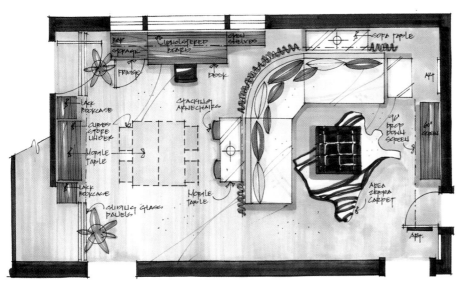

AFTER: Smoky, sultry color with graphic punches of red, gray, and white for contrast creates a sophisticated backdrop for the new entertainment haven. It's a pretty good graduation gift for the two soon-to-be graduates!

SOLUTION

- I started by dividing the big rectangular space into three zones: at one end, an intimate home theater; at the other, space for dancing; and under the windows, a long desk for a super-functional home office that doesn't detract from the home theater.

- Knowing that music and movies and surround-sound speakers would mean a lot of noise, I ripped out the ceiling and insulated it to muffle sound, then put up a new ceiling with wiring for the sound system and lighting. A plush, new, cut-pile carpet also helps absorb sound and warms up the space.

- At the theater end of the room, a big flat-screen TV and media center anchor the focal-point wall. A huge three-piece sectional provides plenty of seating for family and friends, and curtains hung from a curving ceiling-mounted rod wrap this end of the room in a cocoon of sumptuous silk.

- At the other end of the room, I installed a series of sliding mirrored panels that are mounted on ceiling tracks. There's plenty of space for the girls to practice dance moves, and the panels slide back to reveal a storage area—a *pretty* storage area—with shelves for display.

- Under the long, skinny window, I put in a desk with a huge work surface, a message board, and lots of storage for a practical, hardworking home office.

- Color is the big story in this room. I went with the same dark tone for walls, ceiling, and floor to create a cozy yet dramatic environment that's perfect for watching movies and for teenage entertaining. Using the same color on all surfaces moves the eye seamlessly from plane to plane, so you hardly notice the ceiling height or the room's dimensions.

- Dark colors do soak up the light, so lots of lighting is essential. I installed recessed, positionable halogen ceiling fixtures all the way around the room to accent artwork and wash the walls. For some serious cinematic style, I put in a row of inset wall lights about 12 inches above the floor. They'll guide latecomers to the home theater and dance floor but won't cause a glare on the TV screen.

OPPOSITE: Luscious red silk draperies make a dramatic backdrop, dividing the home theater from the dance area beyond. A roomy sectional upholstered in creamy antique velvet brings some life and excitement to the theater zone. A faux zebra rug adds a dash of pattern to contrast with all of the solid colors.

BELOW: In-wall lighting at floor level enhances the home-theater ambience and won't cause a glare on the big-screen TV. What better artwork for a theater than pictures and posters of movie stars? Positionable halogen lights in the ceiling spotlight the art.

STYLE ELEMENTS

- To create the ultimate entertainment haven, I took the room in a dramatic, sophisticated direction with a sultry, smoky charcoal color for the walls, ceiling, and plush, cut-pile carpet. Usually a dark basement is a bad thing, but when you're watching movies, it's perfect. A tip for getting solid paint coverage when you're going dark: Have the paint store tint primer with your paint color. Tinted primer ensures better coverage and will cut down on the number of coats of paint required.

- To brighten things up a bit, I covered the curved sectional in a creamy antique velvet for a decadent 1930s feel. (Note that it matches the color of popcorn!) Decorative pillows in pleated red silk, a gray graphic print, and dark faux snakeskin bring in lots of fun textures to break up the expanse of white.

- Luxurious red silk draperies edged with platinum silk wrap the sectional in a sumptuous cocoon. Ceiling lights are positioned to beam down on the curtains to highlight the texture—it will be so dramatic, the girls might not notice the movie!

- For the big custom-built desk, I used dark, chocolate-color wood, with a slab of gray laminate for the work surface. The desk includes lots of shallow and deep storage to help keep Pamela and the girls organized. A channel-style message center upholstered in creamy fabric picks up the color of the sectional sofa.

RIGHT: To make the mirrored panels, I attached huge mirrors to panels of wood that were hung from the ceiling-mounted track.

BELOW: The mirrored panels in the dance area slide back to reveal a beautiful, dark-wood bookcase and display shelving that balances the television at the other end of the room. A pair of leather-covered cubes can be pulled out for extra seating when there's a crowd.

ABOVE: I painted the window frame black to blend it in with the dark-wood desk and charcoal walls. Dark woven blinds provide privacy at night.

BELOW: Puck lights illuminate the desk's gray laminate surface and an upholstered pin board, where Pamela and the girls can tuck pictures and notes into the channels or pin them in place.

DESIGNED FOR A DRUMMER

CHALLENGE

Andrew and Rachel met and fell in love at a concert, when Andrew was at the drums onstage and Rachel was sitting in the first row. Now, 16 years later, they are happily married with two kids and a dog. Andrew still plays the drums, but only at night (when everyone else wants to sleep) to de-stress after a long day working in the financial industry. Rachel would like to have their dark, very outdated basement renovated as a sound-proof music room for him, a play space for the girls, and a relaxing family room for all of them.

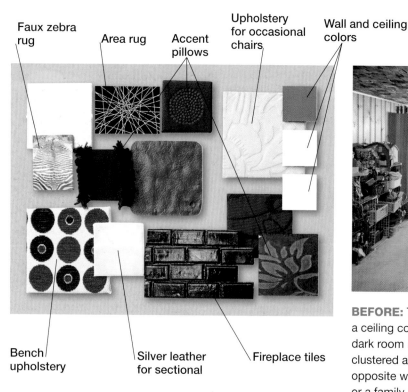

Faux zebra rug · Area rug · Accent pillows · Upholstery for occasional chairs · Wall and ceiling colors · Bench upholstery · Silver leather for sectional · Fireplace tiles

BEFORE: Tongue-and-groove knotty-pine paneling and a ceiling covered with cedar shakes wrapped this long, dark room in rustic Adirondack style. With Andrew's drums clustered at one end and storage bins and shelves lining the opposite wall, the space didn't function well as a music room or a family room.

AFTER: Drum roll, please! Furniture placement breaks up the space into three zones: a bar and beverage area where Andrew can drum to his heart's content; the girls' play area with rock-star–style storage for toys and dress-up costumes; and a TV-and-media zone anchored by a new fireplace.

SOLUTION

- Before I could transform this basement into the ultimate music room, I had to gut the space completely. It was out with the paneling, cedar shakes, and carpet and in with insulation for the walls and a sound-proofing barrier and acoustical drywall on the ceiling.

- For the floor I put down linoleum that looks like industrial concrete. It's surprisingly soft underfoot but very durable.

- The fireplace at one end of the room anchors a big chill-out zone, so I replaced the messy wood-burning fireplace with a gas insert. Hiding the old brick with a new tile facing required smoothing down the uneven surface with a jackhammer so the backer board for the tile could be installed. Talk about percussion!

- For the kids, I carved out a play space with fanciful storage for dress-up costumes and toys.

- For Andrew's music zone, I included a long counter, beverage refrigerator, and bar sink, making this spot a center for entertaining as well as drumming.

- A floating, wall-hung cabinet on the opposite wall displays his stunning collection of snare drums like artwork.

- Lighting is crucial to brightening the basement and making it an appealing place for the whole family. I installed recessed lights overhead along the perimeter and in two rows down the center of the ceiling. Sconces layer more intimate lighting in the bar and chill-out zones.

RIGHT: A silver leather sectional worthy of Elvis carves out a luxurious area for watching TV, enjoying the fire, and relaxing with friends and family. The centerpiece of the kids' play area is a storage cabinet for their toys; crowned with a deep valance and wrapped with draperies, it's a free-standing closet fit for a couple of princesses.

ABOVE: Chrome-and-crystal sconces and recessed fixtures wash the walls, window treatments, and gleaming sectional with light. A graphic black-and-white area rug anchors the lounging zone.

OPPOSITE: Pewter iridescent glass tile sealed with charcoal grout turns the old brick eyesore into a stunning, high-style focal point. I added a mahogany panel to balance the off-center firebox and tied the whole installation together with an extended mantel and hearth.

STYLE ELEMENTS

- One of Andrew's snare drums gave me the jumping-off point for the room. Inspired by the color of the drum, I chose a rock 'n' roll red for one long wall and a silvery blue for the remaining walls. (Red is a challenge—it took seven coats!)

- Picking up the trim on the drum, I chose silver leather upholstery for the very clean-lined sectional—talk about rock-star glam! It's also surprisingly hard-wearing.

- The fireplace is absolutely spectacular, clad in gorgeous iridescent pewter-finished glass tile! Dark grout blends with the tile, and a black quartz mantel and hearth complete the sleek, chic, and totally contemporary treatment.

- I used black quartz counters for the long bar counter too. An under-counter beverage fridge, square under-mounted sink, and modern toggle-style faucet make the entertainment zone totally functional.

- Across from the bar counter, I put in some super-comfy, über-stylish front-row seating: a pair of armchairs upholstered in metallic-look fabric. A pair of glittery pendants and door-height mirrors add light and space-expanding reflections at this end of the room.

- A new bookcase and media center anchor the end wall. I chose a rich mahogany finish for the woodwork here and elsewhere in the room to balance the metallic touches with warmth.

- To keep the redo on budget, I used an easy-to-assemble storage unit for the girls' trinkets, toys, and tiaras. To dress it up in rock-star style, I crowned it with a valance upholstered in white velvet and hung white velvet draperies around it like theater curtains.

- Accent fabrics for pillows include geometrics that look like cymbals and snare drums and a punkerific black fabric that resembles a Mohawk haircut.

- To provide privacy at night, I dressed the windows with woven wood blinds that have a red accent strip—perfect for my color scheme! Hung at ceiling height, they extend below the windowsill to increase the apparent size of the skinny opening.

LEFT: Red and gray carpet tiles add fun color and pattern to the kids' play zone. The princess-worthy storage unit hides a ready-to-assemble cabinet under a ceiling-mounted valance and lush curtains.

BELOW: Plastic bins keep toys organized and make cleanup easy. Hooks mounted on the wall hold dress-up costumes, and when the curtains are drawn, it all disappears!

Chrome-and-crystal sconces with fabric shades illuminate the bar area. The long quartz countertop unites open storage, bar seating, and the bar sink and is perfect for serving a buffet. A faux zebra rug adds fun pattern on the floor.

ABOVE: An under-counter fridge keeps adult and kid beverages handy, and a bar sink with a modern toggle faucet makes cleaning up convenient and easy.

LEFT: Andrew's collection of snare drums is showcased like artwork in this custom-built mahogany-finish floating cabinet. Red leather stools can be moved anywhere they're needed for extra seating.

ABOVE: Occasional chairs upholstered in satiny silver tone-on-tone fabric give Andrew's fans front-row seats for his nightly performances. Matching framed mirrors lean against the wall and enlarge the sense of space, reflecting the light of twinkly pendant lamps.

SPACE FOR SCRAPBOOKING

CHALLENGE

With its knotty-pine paneling, worn carpet, and damaged acoustical-tile ceiling, this 1950s basement puts the "wreck" in rec room! The wood-burning fireplace is too messy to be practical, and homeowners Regan and Steven actually closed it up with cardboard and are using the hearth as a back rest for floor pillows. With a family reunion looming, the couple needs this space to be completely updated to accommodate a crowd. And after the relatives leave, the basement needs to function as an office and scrapbooking studio, as well as a play area for toddler Eden and a place for relaxing and entertaining.

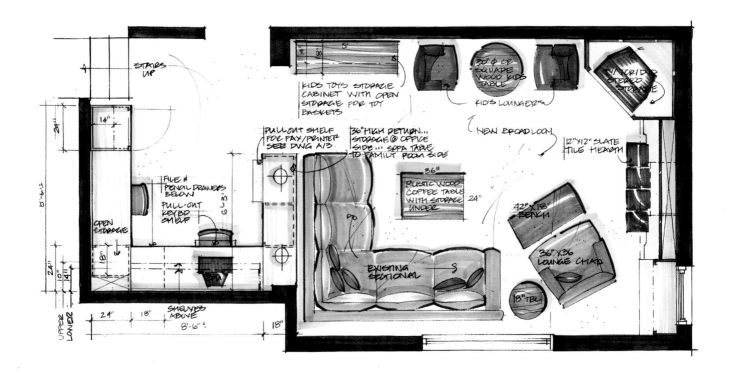

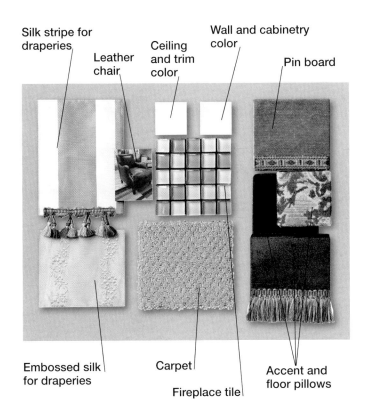

Silk stripe for draperies

Leather chair

Ceiling and trim color

Wall and cabinetry color

Pin board

Embossed silk for draperies

Carpet

Fireplace tile

Accent and floor pillows

BEFORE: A relic of the 1950s, this pine-paneled basement was dark and disorganized, cluttered with kids' toys, and dominated by a huge sectional. The ugly fireplace was being used as a backrest, and the acoustical-tile ceiling was damaged in places.

AFTER: New walls, ceiling, carpet, and lighting bring the basement family room into the twenty-first century. A warm, creamy color lightens and brightens the room, and new, custom built-in cabinetry helps organize the space into functional zones.

SOLUTION

- I started by taking the room back to the studs, ripping out the wood paneling, carpet, and acoustical tiles. I knocked down the ugly angel-stone fireplace surround as well. New drywall on the walls and ceiling, new carpet, and new built-in cabinetry totally transform the space.

- I then divided the multitasking room into zones: an office/work area at the foot of the stairs, a play area, and an entertainment/lounging zone anchored by the fireplace.

- A hardworking peninsula divides the office/work area from the lounging zone. On the lounge side, it serves as a sofa table. On the office side, open cubbies with pull-out shelves are specially designed to keep printers and fax machines handy but out of the way. Custom-built cabinets with open and closed storage wrap the corner, creating a roomy office for Steven and a well-organized work space for Regan.

- At the fireplace end of the room, I designed a whole new surround that incorporates cabinetry under the windows and a long, 22-inch-deep mantel. To reduce the depth of the over-mantel a little, I put up a false wall that accommodates sconces for a more formal, traditional look. I made use of the existing chimney and installed an open-flame gas fireplace. For the heat-proof surround, I chose a glass mosaic tile that picks up the carpet color and adds a little bit of sparkle.

- Beside the fireplace, I built a new corner cabinet to hold a big-screen television and media center and provide more storage.

- Lighting was crucial to brightening the basement and making all the zones function well. In addition to recessed lights that provide overall illumination, I used sconces to focus attention on a new play area for Eden and to highlight the over-mantel. Table and desk lamps supply focused task lighting.

ABOVE: In addition to recessed lights that illuminate Regan's work surface and pin board, puck lights under the shelf shed bright light over Steven's desk area. Regan's pin board is not only perfect for inspiration and ideas but also a way to introduce the softness and pattern of fabric in an area that's otherwise all hard surfaces.

BELOW: Cabinetry defines a hardworking U-shaped space for Regan's scrapbooking (right) and Steven's office (center). The peninsula divides the work area from the lounging area and provides work space and storage the couple can share. I painted the traditional-style cabinetry to blend in with the walls and help brighten the basement.

ABOVE: A new corner cabinet for the television and a new face for the fireplace give the room an entirely new feeling. Adding the corner cabinet made the firebox look off-center, so I boxed in the small window in the opposite corner and added closed storage below to re-center the fireplace.

STYLE ELEMENTS

- A serene cream color on all of the walls and cabinetry creates a light-enhancing, space-expanding feeling in the once-dark basement. For the floor I chose a caramel-color loop-and-cut-pile carpet that's luxuriously plush and durable.

- Regan and Steven wanted the family room to feel warm and welcoming with a touch of traditional style, so I designed all of the cabinetry to incorporate traditional details—crown moldings, recessed panels on cabinet doors, and panel moldings on the side of the corner television cabinet. Even the profile of the new mantel and fireplace surround capture that traditional look.

- For the fireplace surround and new hearth, I chose a delicious glass tile mosaic that incorporates all of the key colors in the space and adds a little bit of a modern touch.

- To make the skinny windows seem bigger and more important, I dressed them with floor-length draperies in a combination of embossed silk framed by cream-and-caramel stripes. Blackout lining protects the silk from the damaging effects of sunlight and gives the draperies more body.

- The couple's big green sectional was one of the few pieces of furniture that stayed. Regan and Steven had been convinced it was too big for the space and needed to go, but I found that simply by flipping its position in the room, it worked perfectly well. To break up the big expanse of solid green, I added throw pillows in accent colors of rust, cocoa, and fawn.

- A new leather club chair and stained-wood coffee table round out the lounging zone, selected for their lived-in, vintage look.

- For Eden, I brought in a painted bookcase to organize her toys and games and hung a super-sized, framed magnet blackboard on the wall where she can draw and be creative. The trio of sconces above illuminates the play area like gallery lighting.

BELOW: Building out the wall above the fireplace created better proportions for the depth of the cabinets on each side. The glass tile surround and hearth bring together the warm, earthy colors in the room.

OPPOSITE: A huge framed blackboard with gallery-style lighting gives Eden her own place to be creative. Big squashy floor pillows and a play table "furnish" the play zone, but when there's a crowd, this area easily turns into extra seating (for young and flexible guests) and a side table. A free-standing bookcase stores toys and games now and will transition to other kinds of storage as Eden grows.

BELOW: The big green sectional had seemed like a liability before, but positioning it against the window wall opens up floor space and retains generous seating—which would be important for that family reunion! Accent pillows in shades of rust, cocoa, and fawn help break up the expanse of solid green.

SEW LOVELY!

CHALLENGE

Yolande and Huy moved from a tiny New York apartment to a huge new home in the suburbs, and they're a little overwhelmed by the space. The sprawling lower level, although finished, is not very functional, but it's full of promise. Yolande is a talented seamstress and would love to have a place to sew. There's plenty of room for the kids to play, but no storage for their toys. And it's a great spot for TV watching, but the room is too cold visually and physically to be inviting. Adding to the challenge is the question of style: Huy likes the clean lines of minimalism and Danish modern furniture. But can modern design and kids coexist?

BEFORE: With beautiful hardwood floors, traditional trim work, and soaring ceilings, the basement was bigger than Yolande and Huy's entire apartment in New York City. The cavernous space had no storage and dwarfed their furniture, and there was no place for Yolande to sew.

AFTER: Now Yolande has a proper sewing table with a clear view of a spectacular new feature wall that incorporates the television they already had and a super-modern fireplace. The low-profile sectional sofa serves as a room divider and offers a ton of seating, so the whole family can snuggle together to watch TV.

SOLUTION

- Yes, modern design and kids can coexist! The secret is to organize and contain all that clutter so the clean lines of modern minimalism can shine through. Cabinetry comes to the rescue here, with lots of beautiful, practical storage for Yolande and the kids as well as a show-stopping new feature wall for the TV/lounging area.

- The feature wall is the first thing you see as you come down the stairs, so I decided on a long, linear, über-modern fireplace surrounded by a spectacular wall of tile. I flanked the fireplace with two columns of display shelving and balanced the fireplace with contemporary custom cabinetry that incorporates the big-screen television into the design.

- On the other side of the room, I put up an entire wall of storage that combines open shelves with closed cabinets to organize all of the kids' toys and games, as well as Yolande's fabrics and sewing supplies.

- On the end wall under the window, I created a work area with a tower of storage, some drawers, and a quartz countertop that serves as a desk. To create a little more intimacy, I stopped all of the cabinetry in the room about 2 feet shy of the 10-foot-high ceilings. It brings the eye down to a more human level.

LEFT: A big, beautiful modern sofa covered in wheat-color linen gets a shot of color with pillows in patterned fabrics. Simple white panels frame the French doors, but to give them some visual weight, I added deep borders of contrasting velvet. Woven wood blinds control light at the windows and add the warmth of natural texture.

ABOVE: A wall of tile frames the new gas fireplace and gives the big room a clear focus. Display towers with puck lights and clear glass shelves add lots of visual interest to the wall, and media-center cabinetry combines storage and display.

ABOVE: A cocoa-and-cream rug anchors the seating area. It overlays a heating pad that plugs into an electrical outlet for toasty toes in the chilly basement. Long, clean lines and lots of light neutrals answer Huy's love of Danish modern design, but a few touches of wood, like the streamlined coffee table, add visual warmth.

STYLE ELEMENTS

- The basement was already finished and needed no structural changes, but I warmed up the stark white walls with a coat of creamy paint.

- For the fireplace surround, I chose a random-format tile that mixes whites and grays for a super-modern pixilated effect. White grout highlights the different shapes of the tile—1 x 1-inch, 1 x 2-inch, and 2 x 2-inch pieces, all fitted together like a puzzle.

- I painted all of the cabinetry cool white to match the white in the tiles. The simplicity of the cabinetry sits in contrast to the texture and pattern of the tile.

- In front of the fireplace and TV, I placed a huge sectional that picks up on the linear look of the feature wall. The sectional and a long, minimalist table behind it act as a room divider, separating the TV zone from the sewing and play areas.

- The basement tends to be cold, so to add a little physical warmth, I put down an anti-slip heating pad under an area rug. The pad plugs into the wall and radiates toasty warmth.

- For Yolande's sewing table, I designed a cool multipurpose pedestal table that butts up to one storage tower. The kids can also pull up chairs and help Mom or work on their own projects.

- To give the wall in Yolande's work area some interest, I put up a subtle wallpaper with a low-contrast, large-scale lattice pattern.

- Puck lights in the cabinets make the most of the display areas and illuminate the desk surface. Over the sewing table I put up a cool, modern light fixture that looks like a spaceship!

- To frame and soften the big, pretty windows in this walk-out basement, I hung simple, ready-made panels customized with a deep velvet border across the bottom.

RIGHT: A pint-size table and beanbag chairs say "kid zone." A wall of closed and open storage keeps all of the kid clutter organized and out of sight.

127

The Great Wall of Storage is a monument to modern design with its clean grid of squares and flat-faced, flush-mounted cabinet doors. That spaceship hovering over Yolande's sewing table is made from a resilient woven stretchy fabric, so it's entirely kid-proof!

LEFT: The sewing corner also accommodates a family office, with a durable, beige quartz countertop, puck lights, and an upholstered pin board for notes and messages. Narrow drawers are perfect for sewing supplies, but they can organize office supplies too.

BELOW: Even minimalism benefits from some softening curves here and there. A low X-leg bench adds a graceful accent under the window overlooking the backyard.

ROOM FOR MUSIC AND MORE

CHALLENGE

This is one very well-lived-in basement family room! It's where teenager Sarah-Grace practices her drums and her brother, Matthew, jams with his band. It's where all of the games and lots of miscellaneous stuff are stored. The back door is the entrance everyone uses, so the area just inside it is crammed with coats and boots and always looks cluttered. Other than an uncomfortable futon, there really isn't anywhere to sit. Mom Denise (and the whole family) would like this room to be an attractive, comfortable place for everyone to relax, including the dog and the bunny!

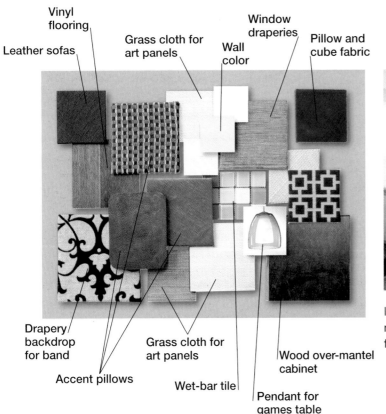

Vinyl flooring
Leather sofas
Grass cloth for art panels
Wall color
Window draperies
Pillow and cube fabric
Drapery backdrop for band
Accent pillows
Grass cloth for art panels
Wet-bar tile
Wood over-mantel cabinet
Pendant for games table

BEFORE: With lots of clutter, no seating, and some overdue maintenance issues, this well-used basement was a long way from a harmonious haven!

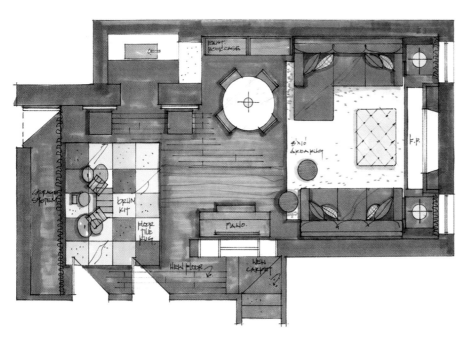

AFTER: Hard-wearing, durable vinyl flooring smoothes out the uneven floor and gives the rich, warm effect of real wood. MDF (medium-density fiberboard) panels papered with cream, wheat, and gold grass-cloth wallpaper frame the doorway to the wet bar. Multipurpose cubes upholstered in teal and topped with satiny pumpkin pillows offer movable seating plus storage. With areas dedicated to music, games, and watching television, the room is ready for rock 'n' roll or relaxation.

ABOVE: A new, walnut-stained cabinet covers the top half of the fireplace and frames a new big-screen TV. Painting the lower half of the fireplace crisp white updates the old brick and gives the room a fresh focus. Silky draperies mask the tiny windows on each side of the fireplace and soften the hard surfaces.

SOLUTION

- The room didn't need to be gutted, but it did need a complete overhaul. The floors were uneven, so I laid down thick vinyl tiles that look like wood. The resilient flooring is ideal for hiding uneven surfaces and gives the appearance and warmth of wood.

- Fresh paint in a warm neutral shade creates an inviting, sophisticated background for new furniture and finishes.

- To organize the space so it can serve multiple purposes, I divided it into three zones: a relaxation zone centered on the fireplace, a music zone, and a wet-bar zone.

- The brick fireplace needed updating to anchor the new relaxation zone. I painted the lower half for a lighter, more modern look and clad the upper half with a wood over-mantel cabinet that frames a new plasma TV.

- The old wet bar was a boring little space, so I pumped up the style with a new counter, a sleek stainless-steel bar sink with a joystick faucet, and beautiful new mosaic tile on the wall above.

- In the music zone, I put up a versatile organizational wall system to tame the clutter of hats, coats, and book bags.

LEFT: The piano stands in front of a large pass-through that connects the family room to a hall leading from the back door to the stairs. Carpet tiles in front of the back door form a stage for the band.

STYLE ELEMENTS

- Comfortable seating was the number one priority for the relaxation zone. I chose two chocolate-brown leather sofas and a matching bumper plus a big, creamy upholstered ottoman to create a cozy seating area anchored by the fireplace and TV. A graphic area rug in pale cocoa and cream pulls the area together and sets off all the solids with a simple, clean pattern.

- To add some softness around the fireplace and give the teeny little windows the illusion of greater size, I hung floor-to-ceiling draperies in a teal, rust, and green silky strié.

- In the music zone, just inside the back door, I created a stage for Sarah-Grace's drums by laying a random pattern of carpet tiles in cream, brown, tan, and two shades of blue. A beautiful flocked linen with a baroque pattern in black on tan creates a backdrop for the drums and hides the organizational system that will catch all the back-door clutter. The fabric is cool enough for rock 'n' rollers but not so crazy that Mom and Dad won't love it too.

- For a punch of color in the wet-bar room, I chose a beautiful blue, teal, gray, and cream mosaic tile that picks up on the colors of the carpet tiles. To create a dramatic frame for the wet bar, I covered two panels of MDF with metallic-backed grass-cloth wallpaper. The panels simply lean against the wall, but they're almost like artwork.

- In the corner beside the wet bar, I placed a small table for games, snacks, or homework, with a gorgeous double-glass pendant above it. The family's existing wood bookshelf got a facelift with mirror added to the back to reflect light and add depth to the room. It's perfect for organizing the games next to the games table.

- I took out the old, oversized recessed lights and installed modern track lights to illuminate both long walls and the music zone.

LEFT: Time to rock 'n' roll! The flocked linen drapery is funky enough for the kids but classic enough for Mom and Dad. The grommet-topped panels are threaded on a sturdy metal pole and can be drawn back to access the wall-mounted storage system that keeps coats, hats, and book bags tidy.

ABOVE: Chocolate leather sofas offer sink-in comfort for family and friends (and the dog). The upholstered ottoman can serve as a coffee table, extra seating, or—when pulled over to the sofa—a place to prop tired feet. Pillows in teal, beige, and cream add punches of color and pattern to keep the expanse of brown leather from overpowering.

OPPOSITE: A pedestal table with its own pendant light fixture stakes out space for games, snacks—and maybe a little homework. I recycled one of the family's bookshelves to store games and books. Mirror attached to the back between the shelves reflects light and creates an illusion of space.

BELOW: I gave the wet bar a major facelift with a sparkly tile backsplash, stainless-steel surface-mounted sink, and crisp white countertop.

MODERN MAKEOVER

CHALLENGE

With their first baby on the way, Marla and Aaron decided to trade in their trendy downtown loft for a house in the 'burbs. This young, hip couple found a gem of 1950s mid-century modern design that has tons of cool, minimalist character, which they love. The basement, however, is another story. A big, rectangular room with dark faux wood paneling, a dingy brick fireplace, acoustical ceiling tiles, and worn-out wall-to-wall carpet, it is retro, but not in a good way. Marla and Aaron would like an updated space where Aaron can rehearse with his band and the couple can entertain guests.

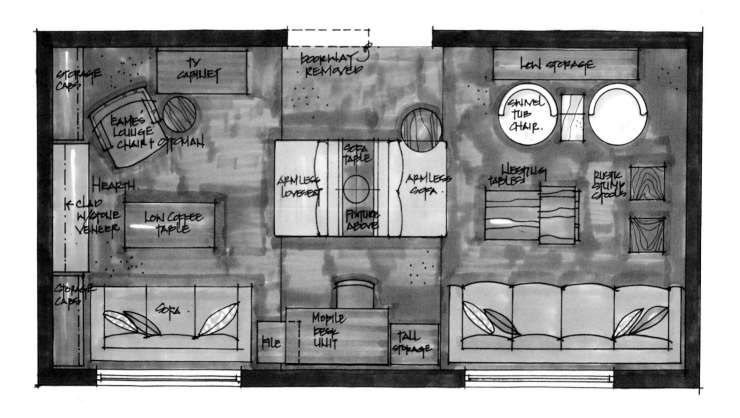

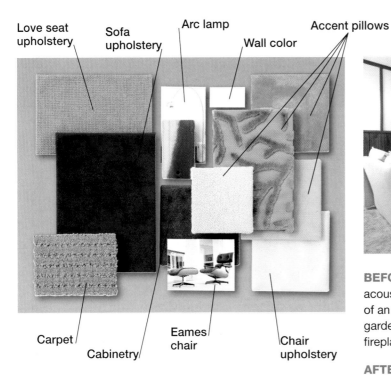

Love seat upholstery
Sofa upholstery
Arc lamp
Wall color
Accent pillows
Carpet
Cabinetry
Eames chair
Chair upholstery

BEFORE: With dark wood paneling, worn-out carpet, and an acoustical-tile ceiling, this basement was in desperate need of an update. Big white panels that must have seemed avant garde at the time just looked odd now, and the pale brick fireplace was dingy and bland.

AFTER: Fresh white walls and ceiling and a durable, caramel-color carpet on the floor give the now-super-stylish basement an instant facelift. Furniture arrangement breaks up the space into two intimate zones with an office nook tucked in between. Dark woven blinds provide privacy at night.

SOLUTION

- Before I could bring this room into the twenty-first century, I had to start almost from scratch. I pulled down the paneling, ripped up the rug, and tore down the ceiling tiles. Along with putting up new drywall and ceiling, I carved out a new doorway for better access. A durable low-pile carpet on the floor warms the space and will be baby- and kid-friendly.

- Because Marla and Aaron want the room to do a little multitasking, I divided it into zones—a rehearsal space for the band at one end, a relaxation and "chilling-out" zone centered on the fireplace at the other, and an unobtrusive office nook in between.

- As the focal point of the relaxation zone, the fireplace wall needed a major overhaul, and I had just the thing—a fabulous cut-stone veneer that's rugged and earthy and looks like a stacked-stone wall. On either side of it, I installed gorgeous new custom cabinetry that stretches from floor to ceiling and provides lots of stylish storage for toys and baby things. (Marla and Aaron will appreciate that very soon!)

- On the wall opposite the fireplace, I put up a huge vinyl-backed photographic mural of birch trees. It anchors the band-rehearsal space and speaks to the colors in the fireplace stone.

- Recessed lighting in the new ceiling washes the walls with light. I installed three fixtures right above the fireplace to make that feature area pop.

LEFT: A photographic mural creates a surprising illusion of depth at the band-rehearsal end of the room. Matching armless love seats sit back to back at the center of the room, dividing the "chill-out" zone from the "rockin' out" zone.

ABOVE: A fabulous stone veneer covers the old brick and anchors the conversation area, which also boasts a new flat-screen TV. For the new built-in cabinetry, I had the doors and drawer fronts constructed with the grain running horizontally, to pick up on the horizontal layers of stone in the fireplace. Long, sleek door handles reflect the clean, minimalist style Marla and Aaron like.

ABOVE: At this hip and happenin' end of the room, a classic 1960s-style arc lamp swoops over the swivel chairs to illuminate a contemporary nesting coffee table. I propped a big mirror on the side wall to reflect more light into the room and to play on the illusion of depth that the mural creates.

STYLE ELEMENTS

- To lighten up this dark basement, I painted the walls and ceiling a crisp birch white. Caramel-color carpet on the floor relates to hues in both the fireplace stone and the mural and helps tie the room together visually.

- Furniture really creates the comfort and style in this room. I chose modern pieces that reflect the best of the 1950s to the 1980s and mixed them with comfy, contemporary seating for a look that is classic yet fresh and stylish. I used a pair of matching armless love seats to divide the room, with a sofa table snugged in between. Then for the "chill-out" zone, I added an iconic Eames lounge chair and ottoman and a modern low-arm sofa upholstered in dark charcoal. A super-stylish clear acrylic coffee table provides a place to rest drinks and snacks but takes up no space visually.

- For Aaron's band buddies, I brought in a couple of retro swivel chairs and a long sofa that's the big-brother version of the sofa at the other end of the room. A shaggy white area rug nods to the 1980s in a fun way, and a funky 1960s-era floor lamp swoops over the seating to illuminate the center of the space.

- On the wall between the two main areas I tucked in a simple, clean-lined black desk with a floating shelf to serve as a small office. A tall bookcase beside it provides more storage.

- To provide privacy at night, I hung black woven-grass blinds over the ribbon windows. I installed the blinds at ceiling height and designed them to fall well below the windows when they're lowered, to create the illusion of greater depth.

RIGHT: A simple desk and chair take up little space visually but provide practical office space for Marla and Aaron. A new version of an iconic 1950s asterisk clock adds a bit of fun retro style.

3 GATHERING SPACES

FAMILY ROOM FACELIFT

CHALLENGE

Once upon a time there was a dark, drab family room trapped in the 1970s. It had dark wood paneling, a massive wall of brick with an unimposing fireplace, a popcorn stucco ceiling, and no lighting to speak of. The furniture was big and bulky, and there was no storage for toys. Its owners, Aimee and Alex, were juggling family and career and had no time to redecorate. But now, with baby number two on the way, Aimee is anxious to transform this room into a bright, contemporary, child-friendly space with lots of storage and room to play. Can I give this story a happy ending? You bet!

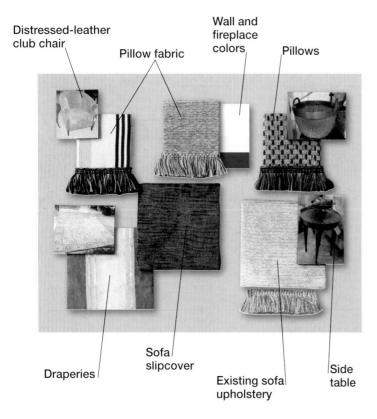

Distressed-leather club chair

Pillow fabric

Wall and fireplace colors

Pillows

Draperies

Sofa slipcover

Existing sofa upholstery

Side table

BEFORE: Dark wood paneling and lots of brick made this family room feel dark and dated. Burlap curtains at the sliding glass door had long since passed their in-style date.

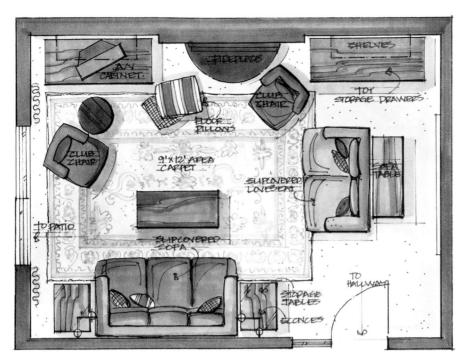

AFTER: Fresh cream-color paint, new lighting, and a high-contrast neutral color scheme take this family room from drab to fab! Now it's a bright and welcoming room for adult entertaining or family play.

SOLUTION

- With the clock ticking (Aimee was eight months pregnant) and a limited budget, paint was my most important tool. A fresh coat of cream paint immediately lightened and brightened the paneling and brick, which brought the room into the twenty-first century! Black heat-resistant paint outlines the fireplace to make it stand out (and to hide soot).

- There were no ceiling fixtures in this room, so I installed pot lights all the way around the perimeter. The popcorn ceiling had to stay, which presented a little bit of a problem: The popcorn finish is a huge headache to patch. My solution? Drill small openings where the ceiling meets the wall, run the wires from the fixture back to the opening, and pull them through and along the ceiling to the next opening. Cover the exposed wires with vinyl crown molding, and voilà! More light, hidden wiring, and new architectural character.

- On the sofa wall, I installed two sconces for reading and task lighting. The wiring is tucked inside an aluminum tube, so we didn't have to drill holes in the wall to pull wiring from a junction box.

- New custom cabinetry for media and toys organizes and hides clutter so the family room can go from play space to adult space in minutes.

- The big, bulky sofas retired downstairs to Guyville, and I brought in a sofa and a love seat that Aimee had inherited from her aunt. The scale of the pieces suits the room better, and the style is more formal than the old recliners. Some additional chairs balance the large seating and make this the perfect space for entertaining, playing with the kids, or just relaxing.

RIGHT: Paint is a quick and economical way to update old brick and wood paneling. I made the fireplace a focal point by painting it with black heat-resistant paint and balancing it with a huge, dramatic mirror. New pot lights direct the eye toward art and furnishings and away from the popcorn ceiling.

OPPOSITE: A two-drawer cabinet hides games and toys. To keep it from tipping forward if babies decide to climb on it, I anchored it to the wall. Black floating shelves with under-shelf lighting make a dramatic staging area for family photos and accents.

ABOVE: High contrast is the secret to a successful neutral color scheme. The dark pewter slipcover on Aimee's inherited sofa stands out boldly against the creamy walls. Artwork, pillows, tables, and drapery fabric repeat that tone to pull the space together. Wall-mounted sconces simply plug into an electrical outlet and require no new wiring.

OPPOSITE: Distressed-leather club chairs are in scale with the room and will only get better with time. I like to layer wall-to-wall carpeting with an area rug—it brings in pattern, reinforces the color scheme, and adds a feeling of richness and luxury.

STYLE ELEMENTS

- At some point, Aimee and Alex plan to open up this room to the kitchen. The neutral wall color I chose will work with anything they might do in their future remodeling. A neutral scheme doesn't have to mean boring, however. The secret to keeping it interesting is high contrast. A scheme of pewter, ebony, and camel works with the existing carpet, which needed to stay, and with Aimee's inherited sofa and love seat, but has enough contrast to give it some drama.

- The drapery fabric pulls the color scheme together. I replaced that old burlap curtain with center-split draperies of striped silk. To allow easy access to the outdoors, I mounted the panels on an 8-foot rod, which allows them to be pulled back from the sliding door.

- All of the fabrics are, needless to say, kid-friendly. I slipcovered Aimee's sofa with a durable pewter fabric to make it stand out against the cream wall. Accent pillows in stripes and prints add contrasting tones to the camel love seat and stack on the floor as cushions for the kids. Distressed-leather club chairs will stand the test of time—and children!

- To provide the storage that the family needs, I had new cherry cabinetry custom-built for each side of the fireplace. The TV and audio-visual equipment go on one side, and deep toy drawers go on the other. Floating shelves above the cabinets provide plenty of room for display and storage.

ASIAN ROOTS

CHALLENGE

Les and Suzanne's exquisite Japanese-inspired backyard garden reflects their Asian heritage (Les is Japanese, Suzanne is Chinese) and is a highlight of neighborhood garden tours. But the sunken family room that overlooks it is anything but serene. A corner full of kids' toys and an eclectic tossed salad of styles—from contemporary and mid-century modern to French country and even Navajo—create a frenetic environment. Les and Suzanne would like to bring the tranquility and order of their garden indoors. My challenge is to balance Asian minimalism with kid-friendly comfort to create a space they can all enjoy.

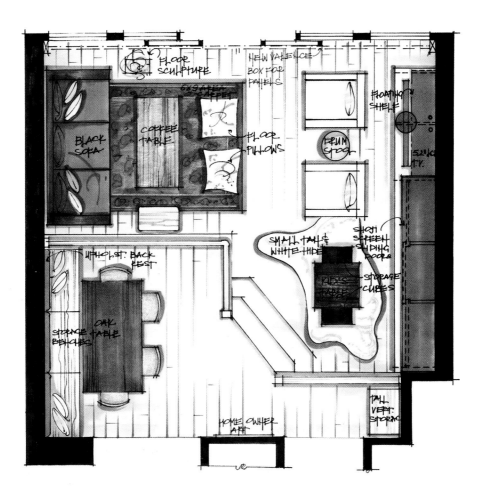

BEFORE: An eclectic mix of furniture styles created a confused and chaotic feeling in this sunken family room. The soaring ceiling dwarfed the storage and seating pieces, and integrated blinds in the glass doors blocked views of the amazing garden outside.

AFTER: Cool blue walls play up the warm honey tones of the wood floors, railings, and trim in the dining area and sunken family room. New cabinetry tames the soaring space and brings it into better scale with the furniture. Asian-inspired lighting emphasizes the Japanese feeling of the room's clean lines.

SOLUTION

- I started by bringing some order and focus to the space with an entire wall of cabinetry—and not just any cabinetry! Doors inspired by shoji screens conceal tons of storage that will hide all of the kid clutter and bring a specifically Japanese feeling to the room.

- The mix of furniture styles was another source of chaos, so I banished the old and brought in new: A deep, super-comfy sofa and a pair of contemporary, low-back armchairs create an adult-space conversation group in the main area, and a low, Chinese-style table and leather ottomans define a play zone for the kids.

- In the dining area overlooking the sunken family room, I built a long banquette that includes storage under the seat. A dark-stained oak pedestal table replaced the old oval one, and new upholstered chairs provide comfortable, grown-up seating for family or guests.

- The wall of windows overlooking the garden was the most important design element in the room, yet the view was blocked by outdated horizontal blinds that were integrated into the double-pane glass. I removed the blinds to open up the view and replaced them with shoji-inspired translucent stacking blinds. When these blinds are retracted, the beauty of the garden comes indoors. When they're closed, the room is bathed in soft light.

RIGHT: Doors that mimic shoji screens (but outfitted with sturdy acrylic panels instead of rice paper) give the new cabinetry a distinctively Japanese look. Drawers below the flat-screen TV conceal cables and media components.

STYLE ELEMENTS

- I used the beautiful honey-toned wood of the floors, railings, and trim as the starting point for the color scheme. I chose a stormy blue-gray for the walls to balance the warm wood tones, with accents in black and cream for a serene mood.

- For the wall of new cabinetry, I designed very minimalist lower cabinets stained a golden tone to go with the floor. The upper cabinets and floating shelves are ebony to bring in the Japanese feeling. For the shoji-screen doors, I knew that rice paper and kids' play wouldn't mix! White acrylic panels give the cabinet doors the effect of rice paper but are durable and kid-proof.

- Lantern-style light fixtures made of cherry wood and rice paper bring a distinctively Asian look to the room. I added matching sconces above the new sofa for a more intimate feeling and installed recessed lights around the living room and dining area to wash light down the walls at night.

- Fabrics reinforce the color scheme: Charcoal velvet on the 42-inch sofa picks up the ebony color of the cabinetry, and soft silvery-blue accents in pillows and art complement the golden tones of the wood. Cream upholstery on the new armchairs ties to the cream-color fabric on the new dining chairs. The area rug pulls together the cream and blue and brings in the soft tan tones of natural wood. For the banquette in the dining area, I opted for a tough, kid-proof black vinyl product with a faux lizard texture.

- To add some graphic interest to the walls, I applied some really cool "wall tattoos." They give the look of stenciling without the work or mess of painting: Just rub on the design and pull away the paper or vinyl backing. I used a cherry branch design in the family room and swimming koi on the dining room wall to bring home the Asian theme.

ABOVE: A rub-on graphic of cherry blossom branches brings the garden inside and adds interest to the high wall. Pagoda-style sconces create an intimate glow in the sofa nook.

OPPOSITE: Suzanne, Les, and their two little daughters can all sink back on this delicious three-seater sofa and watch TV. In Japanese design, beauty is in the details—like the intricate detail in the floor pillows inspired by a kimono.

BELOW: The clean, straight lines of the new pedestal table and dining chairs capture the minimalist style that Les and Suzanne wanted. The built-in banquette makes more efficient use of the space and includes concealed storage.

OPPOSITE: Fanciful koi in charcoal, silver, and gold swim over the dining room wall. Recessed fixtures call attention to the graphics and the light-reflecting Chinese-style mirrors.

ABOVE: The girls have their own play area, with a Chinese-style table and faux leather ottomans. The ottomans double as storage bins, and there's lots more storage for games and toys in the drawers and cabinets nearby.

BELOW: Super-minimalist armchairs book-end the conversation area but stay clear of the traffic path to the outdoors. With the integrated blinds removed from the windows, that glorious view is always available, but if Suzanne and Les want to filter strong summer sun, they can simply draw the translucent vertical blinds across.

UPDATED NEIGHBORHOOD PUB

CHALLENGE

Gerry Dee is a stand-up comedian who admits he gets his best material from family and friends. That's one reason he is eager to do something about the basement in the house he and his wife and baby daughter recently moved into. The only "improvement" he's had time to make in the odd, empty space was to paint one wall a very bold green—sort of an homage to his grandfather and golfing. That was enough to convince him—and his wife—that they need my help to turn this space into a comfortable family room that can host long evenings of conversation and laughter and keep the punch lines coming.

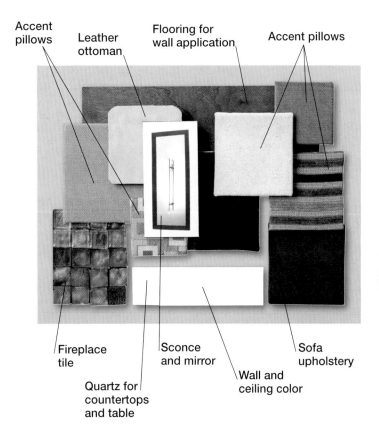

Accent pillows
Leather ottoman
Flooring for wall application
Accent pillows
Fireplace tile
Quartz for countertops and table
Sconce and mirror
Wall and ceiling color
Sofa upholstery

BEFORE: The basement was a funny space, and not in a ha-ha way! The corner fireplace didn't actually work, and the bulkheads made the ceiling feel very low. Gerry's lone effort at decorating—that long green wall—convinced him to call in a professional.

AFTER: Light neutral walls and ceiling focus attention on the spectacular feature wall, where shimmering tile frames an electric fireplace. Warm wood planks clad the walls in a stylized interpretation of paneling. A plump plum-color sectional divides the bar area from the TV/lounging area and offers a ton of seating for Gerry and friends.

ABOVE: My inspiration was an old English pub, but I interpreted it in a modern way with a sleek quartz table in the bar area and a modern sectional in the TV area. To contrast with all of the solid upholstery, I anchored the TV area with an exquisite area rug in soft, muted tones of plum, cream, and caramel.

SOLUTION

- Gerry wants the family room to be a cozy, comfortable place his wife and daughter can enjoy while he was on the comedy circuit and a gathering spot for family and friends when he is at home. I started by dividing the long space into two zones, with a beautiful bar area anchored by a fireplace at one end of the room and a lounging area focused on the television at the other.

- The old corner fireplace didn't have enough presence to be a feature (and it didn't work), so I tore it out and replaced it with an electric fireplace that has one of the most realistic fires on the market. I had to build out the wall slightly to accommodate the unit. Mounting it in the center of the wall means it's visible from anywhere in the room—a stunning focal point that instantly says, "Sit down and stay awhile."

- In front of the fireplace, I positioned a heavy quartz bar table that's sleek and contemporary.

- New custom bar cabinetry along the walls on either side of the room includes a built-in bar fridge and a sink.

- A big sectional provides tons of seating and acts as a room divider between Gerry's Pub and Gerry's TV Room.

LEFT: The laundry room is on the other side of the wall, so I was able to pull plumbing through to this side and install a bar sink. Wood cabinetry topped with thick, creamy quartz builds on the visual warmth of the wood wall. Puck lights on the underside of the floating shelf illuminate the countertop.

ABOVE: In this small space, clear acrylic chairs virtually disappear, keeping the focus on the beautiful tile and the creamy quartz table. Dramatic chrome sconces have a super-long base that helps push the eye upward to make the ceiling seem higher. Wood floor planks laid horizontally add unexpected warmth and are an unusual take on paneling.

ABOVE: Sconces mounted through tall mirrors balance those at the other end of the room and add the much-needed illusion of height. Instead of enclosing the television in wooden cabinetry, I opted for this simple solution: a row of open cubbies above the television balanced by the low cabinet that holds the TV.

STYLE ELEMENTS

- The room is actually fairly small, so I wanted to turn that into an advantage and create a cozy, intimate feeling. But I also needed to maximize light, because the room has no windows. A fresh coat of light neutral paint on all of the walls, ceiling, and bulkheads unifies and opens the space.

- A few recessed ceiling lights were already in place, so I added accent lighting at each end of the room with dramatic chrome sconces. At the TV end, the sconces are installed through ceiling-height framed mirrors that flank the television. Tall mirrors are one of my favorite space-expanding tricks—they reflect light and views and make any room feel much larger.

- The really eye-catching feature of the room is the fireplace, so I needed a show-stopping tile. I decided on gorgeous iridescent glass tiles laid in bands of cream and copper, with notes of plum and caramel.

- On each side of the fireplace, I clad the wall with rustic wood flooring planks laid horizontally. It's a totally unexpected application that adds lots of warmth.

- For fabrics, I looked to the tile. A rich, plum-color fabric pulls out one of the tones in the tile and upholsters the sectional. Yummy caramel leather covers a chunky, button-tufted ottoman. Pillows in caramel, plum, copper, gray, and cream add some lively color and pattern.

- For wall art, I came up with a super-cool presentation that adds both aesthetics and light. Digital images representing "the history of the microphone" are printed on thin acrylic panels that are installed in frames and mounted over lights, like light boxes. The lights make the images glow and add to the ambient light in the room as well. When the lights are turned off, the prints look like black-and-white photos.

RIGHT: On a wall with no furniture, hanging prints lower than eye level fill the space comfortably. The mirror reflects the crushed-velvet curtain that I hung over the doorway—so Gerry can make a suitably grand entrance!

ABOVE: This electric fireplace has the most realistic flame on the market. The unit is super-shallow, so it doesn't need much wall depth for installation. I like to lift fireplaces off the floor for safety reasons, if you have little ones around, and for decorative reasons, so they can be enjoyed from anywhere in the room.

LEFT: With a built-in bar fridge and plenty of storage space, Gerry and his wife can host cocktail parties down here or whip up some popcorn and watch TV.

JUST WHAT THE DOCTOR (AND NURSE) ORDERED

CHALLENGE

As full-time medical professionals with two young children, Ginny and Oleg juggle work shifts, kids' activities, and family life, so weekends are precious for much-needed "together" time. They love their new home, but the one room that would be perfect for a family gathering space is the unfinished below-ground basement. It's cold, dark, and so creepy that the kids won't go down there by themselves! Ginny and Oleg would love to have a cozy, warm, finished space where they can watch TV together, read stories, and play games—a happy heart of the home.

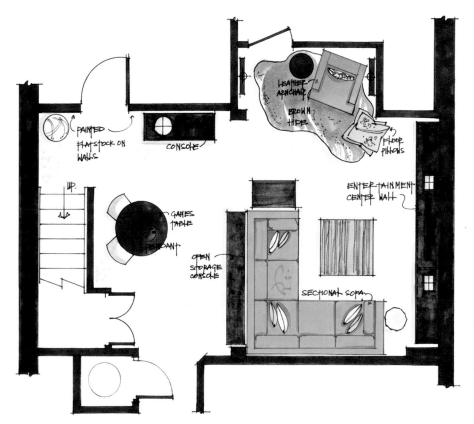

AFTER: The cure for cold and creepy is warm color and natural texture. Chocolate grass-cloth wallpaper on some walls and sunny, butter-yellow paint on others instantly ups the cozy factor. Of course, finishing the ceiling and encasing the ductwork in a broad bulkhead also helps!

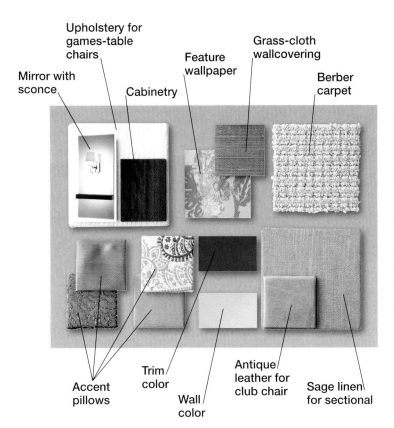

Mirror with sconce

Upholstery for games-table chairs

Cabinetry

Feature wallpaper

Grass-cloth wallcovering

Berber carpet

Accent pillows

Trim color

Wall color

Antique leather for club chair

Sage linen for sectional

BEFORE: The unfinished basement was big, dark, cold, and creepy, with a concrete floor, open ceiling, and exposed ductwork. Ginny and Oleg and their two young children watched television down here on weekends, but otherwise, the kids avoided the place.

SOLUTION

- First I ordered a dose of drywall for the ceiling, with a bulkhead to enclose the ductwork and a new wall to close off the furnace room.

- To warm up the cold concrete floors, I had the perfect prescription: a unique radiant heat system of electric pads that simply roll out on the floor like a carpet pad. For some touchy-feely tactile warmth, I laid hard-wearing, creamy wall-to-wall Berber carpet on top.

- Next, I divided the room into two zones: a living area and a games area. To anchor the living area, I created a feature wall with a large-scale floral wallpaper and cabinetry that stretches across the entire wall. The cabinetry system includes floor-level cabinets that hold the big-screen TV and a row of wall-mounted cabinets for overhead storage.

- The cure for darkness is light and mirrors. I installed a few recessed lights, but relied mostly on track lights mounted on the back of the bulkhead—they're less work to put up and easier on the budget. Puck lights in the wall cabinets and accent fixtures around the room also brighten the space.

- In a nook beside the stairs, I established a games area with a round table and a beautiful light fixture that will be the first thing the family sees when they come down the stairs.

RIGHT: Wallpaper is a relatively inexpensive way to create a stunning feature wall. This floral inspired the colors for the room and provides an interesting contrast to the sleek, contemporary look of the cabinetry. Puck lights installed in the floating cabinets wash light down the wall and help brighten the dark basement.

ABOVE: Perfect for family cuddling and movie nights, a contemporary sectional covered in sage linen divides the room into a living area and a games area. Mixing a few antique pieces, like the pine table, with modern ones adds personality and depth to a room.

STYLE ELEMENTS

- The quickest way to warm up a chilly space is with color and texture. Color comes from the floral wallpaper and makes its way into the rest of the room by way of chocolate grass-cloth wallpaper, buttery paint, and a gorgeous floral pattern in chocolate, butterscotch, and sage.

- Texture adds tactile warmth by way of the natural-fiber grass-cloth wall covering and the Berber carpet. With natural-fiber wallpapers, you can't really hide the seams, so the best approach is to overlap the panels a bit and make a double cut through both. It's also a good idea to paint the baseboard before putting up the wallpaper. If you let the color extend onto the wall, any slight imperfections where the wallpaper meets the baseboard won't be noticeable.

- Dark, coffee-color cabinetry and occasional tables add richness and more visual warmth. The sleek, contemporary floating cabinets for the feature wall emphasize a clean-lined, modern look. The dark cabinetry plays against a large-scale traditional floral for dramatic contrast and character that liven up the room.

- A deep, large, L-shaped sectional in sage linen is perfect for a family of four to cuddle up for movie night or reading. For a coffee table, I chose an antique, distressed-pine piece. Its patina is yet another way to bring in visual warmth and play off the modern cabinetry and sofa.

- In the nook beside the furnace room, I placed a lounge chair upholstered in a yummy butterscotch antique leather. On the wall, a mirror and sconce provide reading light and create the effect of a window (see page 180).

- Ginny likes to keep things neat and organized, so I knew she would love the ready-to-assemble black console I found to go behind the sofa. I topped it with glass for a custom look.

RIGHT: A beautiful chrome-and-crystal chandelier hangs over the games table. Wood battens applied to walls create the effect of traditional recessed panels, giving the walls more character and texture.

OPPOSITE: A super-comfy club chair upholstered in buttery gold antique leather turns one corner into a reading nook. A sconce mounted through a tall mirror illuminates the corner and, along with a painting of birch trees, creates the effect of windows in this windowless space.

BELOW: This ready-to-assemble console is the perfect height for a sofa table and also acts as a room divider. Open cubbies hold an assortment of boxes that stash games, magazines, and other paraphernalia, keeping the look tidy and organized.

CHAMPIONSHIP SEASON

CHALLENGE

Sean and Cara live, eat, and breathe sports. Sean is a professional football player and an NFL Super Bowl champ, and Cara is a former National Women's Hockey Team member. During Sean's off-season, they run a football camp, and they're raising their two young daughters to be sports lovers as well. Their basement is a very purple space that until now has been a playroom for the girls. Sean and Cara would like to move the toys elsewhere and turn the basement into a comfortable grown-up space for entertaining. And they'd like to have a way to display their sports memorabilia tastefully.

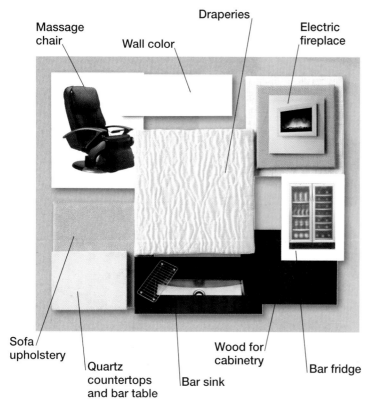

Massage chair
Wall color
Draperies
Electric fireplace
Sofa upholstery
Quartz countertops and bar table
Bar sink
Wood for cabinetry
Bar fridge

BEFORE: Bright purple walls and leftover furniture were fine for the children's play space, but Cara and Sean were ready to move the girls' toys to another room and reclaim this space for entertaining family and friends. Sean is fond of the slouchy sofa, but Cara thinks it's frumpy. Looks like I might have to play referee!

AFTER: Displaying colorful sports memorabilia without creating a sports-bar look is a matter of balance. Dark cabinetry and flooring and light, creamy walls, upholstery, and draperies let the bright colors of the uniforms tell the story. To make sense of the awkward window, I flanked it with display cabinets and covered the window and remaining wall with creamy draperies.

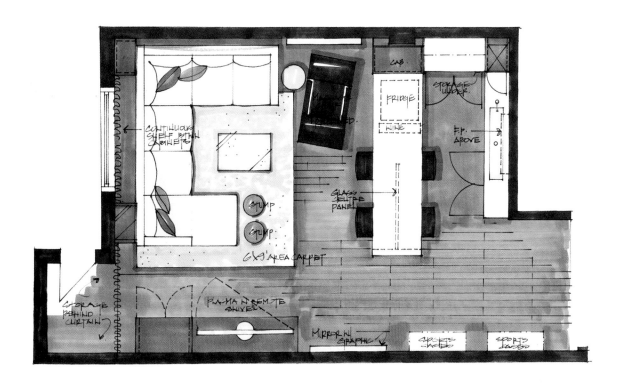

CONTINUOUS SHELF BEHIND ARCHITES

CAB

FRIDGE

STORAGE UNDER

WINE

F.P. ABOVE

GLASS JELLYE PANEL

STUMP

STUMP

6X9' AREA CARPET

STORAGE BEHIND CURTAIN

PLASMA N REMOTE SHELFE

MIRROR IN GRAPHIC

SPORTS CASES

SPORTS LOGOS

SOLUTION

- I kicked off the project by dividing the room into two zones: a bar area and a sports area. I accessed the adjacent furnace room for water to bring in a wet bar at one end of the space. The bar cabinetry provides all of the storage Sean and Cara will need, so I used the remaining area for an extended counter and bar stools to encourage people to gather.

- A super-cool 42 x 6-inch sink squeezes maximum function and style into minimum space in the bar. An under-counter fridge with different temperature zones for different types of beverages anchors one end of the counter.

- For the countertops, I chose indestructible quartz. They are bee-yoo-tiful and weigh a ton!

- Sean and Cara will be watching important games down here, so I designed a media center with a big, important TV. It pivots at the push of a button, angling toward the bar or facing the sofa. How cool is that?

- I replaced the old carpet with new pre-finished wood flooring. It's much more forgiving for parties than light-color carpet, and it's kid-proof too.

- In addition to the bar cabinetry and media center, I designed tons of custom cabinetry for displaying all of Sean and Cara's sports memorabilia. Tall, open cabinets flank the window, and additional glass cabinets rest on the media center and the bar counter and hang on the wall.

- Every bar needs a fireplace, and I found the perfect slim-line electric model for the wall above the sink. It's the fastest fireplace installation you can imagine: Hang it on the wall, feed the cord through the wall, and plug it into the outlet on the other side!

LEFT: In a super-easy installation, a slim-line electric fireplace simply mounts on the wall and plugs into an outlet. A skinny bar sink with the faucet at one end is perfect for bringing wet-bar capabilities into a small space.

ABOVE: With a big U-shaped sectional set into one corner and chairs at the bar, the basement now has plenty of seating to accommodate a crowd. Layers of light banish the basement blues: Recessed fixtures in the ceiling provide ambient light, puck lights illuminate display cases, sconces add an intimate glow, and a super-cool chandelier adds unexpected sparkle.

BELOW: The media center features the all-important big-screen TV and a custom display case, complete with in-cabinet lighting to spotlight the display and mirror backing to reflect light into the room. The tall, wall-mounted mirror features an image of Sean that I turned into a graphic art piece.

OPPOSITE: Wall-mounted display cabinets show off uniforms and mementos from Sean's and Cara's athletic careers. I kept the color palette in the room neutral to play up the importance of their memorabilia.

STYLE ELEMENTS

- The big story in this room is the couple's athletic careers, and the uniforms provide the color. I played up that color by playing it down elsewhere. Cool cream on the walls, ceiling, and draperies and vanilla-cream quartz for the counters balance the dark tones of the display cases, media center, and bar cabinets.

- A U-shaped sectional provides lots of seating in a small space. Covered in a soft, luxurious pale sand color, it's the perfect combination of sink-in comfort for Sean and modern style for Cara.

- To make sense of the off-center window, I extended the drapery across the entire space between the open display cabinets and continued it across the wall on the other side of the cabinetry.

- I like to use mirrors to reflect light and increase the illusion of space, and for Sean and Cara, I came up with something unique. I took their photos and created my own artistic interpretation, then had a specialty company convert the images into life-size graphic art pieces on vinyl film. In a delicate and time-consuming process, the film is applied in multiple layers to the mirror to produce the final image.

- To display the sports uniforms and memorabilia, I arranged them in a combination of custom and ready-made dark wood cases. Precious items—including a little thing we call the Super Bowl ring—stay dust-free and safe behind glass doors.

- To brighten the basement room, I added recessed fixtures in the ceiling and included puck lights in the display cases. Over the bar, I hung a super-modern linear chandelier that adds a little sparkle and style—definitely not your typical sports-bar fixture!

- As a surprise for Sean, Cara requested a massage chair. I found a super-stylish, super-deluxe chair that can be programmed for customized leg, shoulder, and back massages. Everyone is going to want to sit in it!

THE ULTIMATE GUYS' SPACE

CHALLENGE

Neil, a singer, songwriter, and music producer, is a single dad raising two boys. They love to camp, fish, and do just about anything in the great outdoors, but when they are at home, they don't have a place to just hang out together, watch TV, and play music. Fortunately, the basement is basically empty except for some unused furniture and stacks of boxes. The ceiling is low and the room is dark, but it is the perfect place for a "men's den." Super-dad and super-musician Neil asked me to turn it into the ultimate guy space as a gift for his boys.

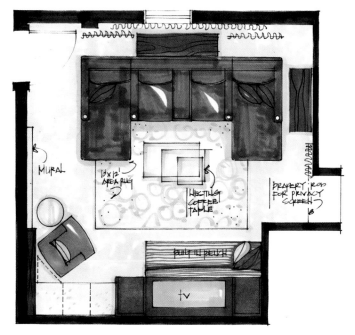

BEFORE: A basically bland, unused space, the basement was a carpeted catchall for odds and ends of furniture and stacks of boxes. The only natural light came from a window in the back door and a dinky little window in the adjacent wall.

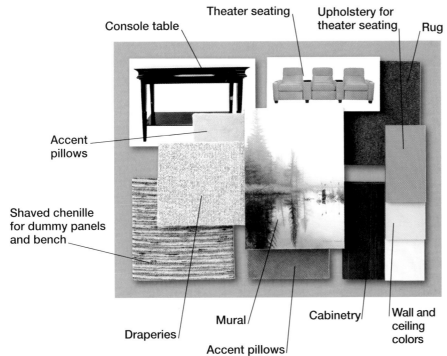

Console table

Theater seating

Upholstery for theater seating

Rug

Accent pillows

Shaved chenille for dummy panels and bench

Draperies

Mural

Accent pillows

Cabinetry

Wall and ceiling colors

AFTER: With my starting point as the guys' love of the outdoors, I used a beautiful photo of a peaceful, serene lake in the mist to establish the theme and guide the color choices. Smoky blue walls and upholstery wrap the room in a soothing cocoon of color that sets the mood for kicking back and watching movies.

SOLUTION

- Men—and boys—love their big-screen TVs, so of course I had to plan for a 60-inch flat-screen TV. It's showcased in custom-built cabinetry that fills the entire wall and includes a snack center with a beverage fridge.

- A theater-size TV means theater-style seating! I found the coolest seating options: Two stretched-out chaises flank two motorized recliners that lean back at the touch of a button. The chair arms have places for popcorn, drinks, and the remote control.

- In front of the TV, I built in a long, fully upholstered bench that's really like a built-in sofa. It will provide extra seating when the boys have friends over.

- To bring some light into the room, I installed a track system with halogen lights and framed the theater seating with pendants. For accent lighting, I recessed puck lights into the bulkhead to shine down on the cabinetry and tucked the same type of fixture into the corner of the side wall to shine along the length of the shelves. Both areas—the bulkhead and the exterior wall—were too shallow for ordinary puck lights, so I used small ones instead.

RIGHT: An entire wall of custom cabinetry fills the space under the bulkhead. Open shelves frame the big-screen TV (an absolute must for any "men's den"), and closed cabinets below provide more storage. I also included a beverage fridge and snack center, with floating shelves above for storage or display.

ABOVE: A pair of chaises and two motorized recliners add up to one super-luxurious home theater! Gauzy draperies completely disguise the small window behind the chairs. Pendants with pleated paper shades bring light down into the room, and a mirror above the console table helps bounce light back into the room.

STYLE ELEMENTS

- To design the ultimate guy space, I needed a theme as my jumping-off point for colors and fabrics. Neil and his boys love fishing and being outdoors, so for a big-impact focal-point feature, I had a painting of a north-woods lake photographed and enlarged to make a big mural. I built out the wall slightly and wrapped the mural over the edge to give it the look of a wall-size canvas.

- I wanted the room to feel both rugged and peaceful. For the walls, I chose the color "Winter Lake," which pulls out a smoky blue-gray tone from the mural. Cabinetry in rich, dark wood speaks to the dark trees in the mural and grounds the low-contrast color scheme.

- Stainless-steel laminate on the countertop of the snack center blends with the walls. A double-decker steel coffee table, on the other hand, has a warm, burnished finish that harmonizes with the wood.

- The cool, misty colors of the mural inspired the gray flannel upholstery for the theater seating. For the bench and drapery panels, I found an amazing gray shaved chenille that looks like tree bark—perfect! A wing chair covered in butterscotch leather gives Neil a good place to sit and compose tunes on his guitar.

- To increase the apparent size of the window, I hung gauzy, misty draperies flanked by dummy panels made from the gray chenille. A matching panel hangs over the entrance from the hall as a privacy panel to darken the room when the guys are watching movies.

BELOW: I built out the wall slightly to create a floor-to-ceiling, 73-inch-wide support for the photo mural so that it would seem like a giant canvas. A geometric area rug in dark, woodsy tones layers over the existing wall-to-wall carpet to ground the seating area.

ABOVE: Custom cabinetry frames the super-size TV and includes space for stereo speakers and storage for DVDs. The custom-built bench expands the seating options when the guys have friends over for playing music or just chilling out.

OPPOSITE: An under-counter fridge keeps cold sodas and water handy for movie nights. Puck lights installed in the end wall throw light horizontally along the shelves and illuminate the snack center.

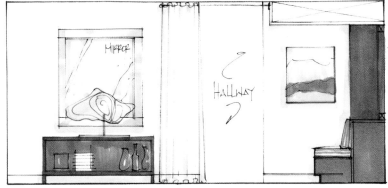

CASUAL COTTAGE STYLE

CHALLENGE

Fourteen-foot ceilings, expansive country-like views, and a fireplace—sounds like a great room! But it's not. That high ceiling is paneled in dark wood, and the big, bulky hearth eats up a lot of valuable floor space. A massive wall of drab brick soaks up all of the natural light. Oversized furniture makes the room feel cramped, and a mountain of plastic bins filled with Cindy's doll collection and the kids' toys almost blocks those country-like views. Cindy and John, who are of Japanese descent, would love to have a room that's fresh, bright, and more contemporary—a cozy cottage feel with a touch of Japanese inspiration.

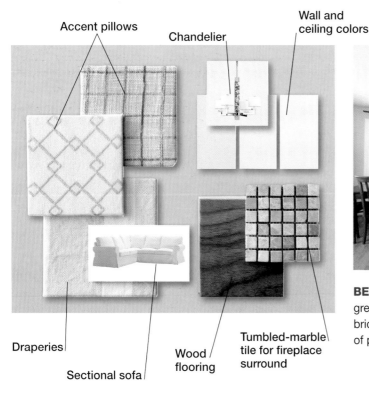

Accent pillows

Chandelier

Wall and ceiling colors

Draperies

Sectional sofa

Wood flooring

Tumbled-marble tile for fireplace surround

BEFORE: Cindy and John's great room was anything but great. The soaring, wood-paneled ceiling and overpowering brick wall made the room feel dark and outdated, and stacks of plastic bins cluttered the space.

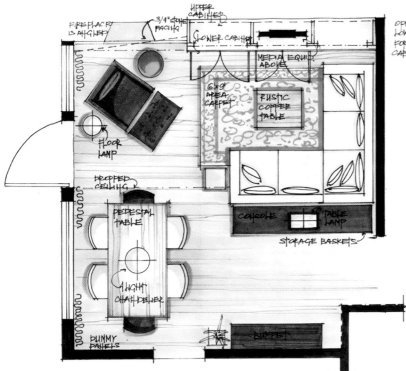

AFTER: Now this is a great room! Paint and new built-in cabinetry totally transform the character of the space. A new fireplace mantel and surround update the look to fresh cottage style, and new furnishings are in better scale with the room.

SOLUTION

- To take this room from grim to great, I started with the hard surfaces. The huge hearth had to be jack-hammered out to free up floor space, and the surface of the brick wall had to be ground smooth to eliminate the drippy mortar. Then I drywalled over the brick, leaving only the chimney stack exposed.

- A beautiful new mantel with traditional-style panel moldings and a tumbled-marble tile surround turn the eyesore of a fireplace into a focal point. For a cleaner, more efficient heat source, I converted the fireplace to gas with an insert.

- To tame the soaring ceiling and give it more architectural character, I installed batten moldings on the fascia and faux beams on the ceiling. Painting the chimney stack, ceiling, fascia, and mantel the same light ivory color immediately lightened and brightened the entire space.

- The old wood flooring had too much yellow in it for the fresh cottage style I had in mind. A mid-tone walnut with a hand-scraped look has the cooler, darker browns that ground the new color scheme with a rustic feel.

- To solve Cindy and John's storage and display problems, I said bye-bye to the plastic bins and hello to big, beautiful cabinetry. A whole new wall of custom-built cabinets converts the wasted space of that expanse of brick into super-efficient storage and display.

OPPOSITE: A completely reworked fireplace is now a beautiful and functional focal point for the room. Removing the hearth made space for a comfortable fireside chair and ottoman, with a floor lamp for reading. Painting the brick chimney lightened and brightened the room while paying homage to the rustic character of the brick.

BELOW: Faux beams on the ceiling and battens on the fascia give the soaring space architectural character. Light ivory paint unifies all of the surfaces and incorporates the new cabinetry into the architecture. I used natural-stained wood for the cabinet shelves to achieve the rustic cottage look that Cindy and John wanted.

STYLE ELEMENTS

- Fabrics and furnishings drive home the casual, family-friendly feeling that Cindy and John wanted. I looked to the outdoors, to the view that attracted them to this house, for color inspiration and chose a soft, wispy sky-blue for the walls and a breezy, natural palette of linen, sand, and celery for the fabrics.

- A new L-shaped sectional slipcovered in humble, washable cotton has room for everyone to sit together. The sandy color of the slipcover perfectly matches the tumbled-marble tile surround on the fireplace—a nice color connection that pulls the room together.

- With the hearth gone, there's room for a fireside chair and ottoman upholstered in durable distressed leather. I chose a dark chocolate for the leather to tie in with the floor color and balance all of the cool, light hues in the room.

- I painted the new built-in cabinetry the same ivory as the walls, fascia, and brick to blend it in with the architecture and brighten the room. For a rustic touch, I used natural wood for the open shelving and chose some very cool hardware that looks like weathered wood. Mirror backing behind the shelves reflects even more light into the room.

- To frame the windows and the beautiful view, I hung simple grommet-topped draperies made from an elegant blue-and-cream stripe. (A tip for working with stripes: Whichever stripe you put the grommet in is the one that will disappear when the draperies are pulled back. I wanted to emphasize the light-blue stripe, so I put the grommets in the cream stripes.) Woven-grass blinds bring in some natural texture and provide light control.

- In the dining area, I kept Cindy and John's old table and hung a beautiful new mother-of-pearl light fixture over it. The fixture combines natural texture and contemporary style and subtly picks up the colors in the room. New upholstered chairs update the dining area with modern style—and modern comfort!

- The dropped ceiling over the dining area is concrete, so I couldn't put in recessed ceiling lights. Instead, I installed track lighting to provide positionable illumination.

- In the living area, I replaced the old ceiling fan with a new, dark-toned fan that falls 36 inches below the ceiling. This visually drops the ceiling to a cozier height and allows the fan to create better air circulation where it actually matters—down where people are sitting.

RIGHT: A terrific ready-to-assemble storage piece does triple duty as a sofa table, room divider, and clutter-control center. The open cubbies and woven-wicker bins organize the children's toys and games, so there's no more need for plastic bins!

ABOVE: An L-shaped sectional slipcovered in washable cotton provides plenty of comfortable seating for the whole family, but is in better scale with the room than the old, oversized seating. The wall of cabinetry solves the old "bin there, done that" problem with tons of space to display Cindy's collection of Japanese dolls and art.

ABOVE: The great room is the first area guests see when they come in the front door, so it really sets the style for the whole house. The soft blue wall color continues from the seating area to the entry. Track lights can be positioned to highlight the buffet and the living area.

LEFT: Placing the dining table parallel to the big window takes advantage of the beautiful view. A new espresso-color buffet stores table linens and dining room necessities. I painted the dining room wall a soft celery color for a touch of warm contrast to the soft blue used everywhere else.

LOG-CABIN LIVING

CHALLENGE

Fran and Jeff's dream home started life as a tiny log cabin and grew over time into a large, modern, but somewhat haphazardly arranged house. What they call their great room still has the log-cabin vibe, with its wood-paneled walls and enormous stone fireplace, but the super-tall windows are all different heights, and the only lighting comes from a huge wagon-wheel chandelier—a lingering bit of the Wild West! The couple want to keep the log-cabin feeling, but they long for something a little more stylish and upscale, a truly "great room" to share with family and friends.

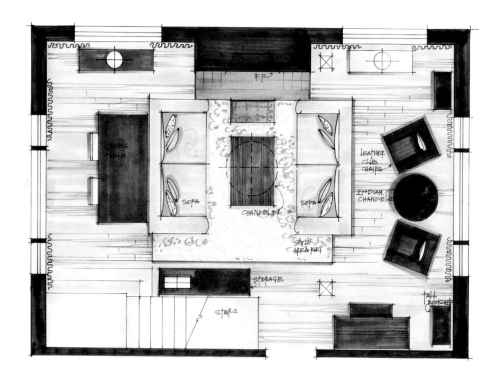

BEFORE: Soaring windows, soaring ceiling, soaring wall of stone—this wood-paneled great room was all about dramatic scale and height. It was almost too much of a good thing because the furniture was dwarfed by the scale, and the wide-plank paneling, while glorious, made the room dark in spite of all the windows. And then there was that wagon wheel hovering overhead . . . .

AFTER: New furniture that's in scale with the room and a huge mirror above the fireplace help bring the vast space into balance. The paneling and stone that give the room its "lodge" feeling are still there, but new lighting and a color scheme that coordinates with the stone take the look from weathered and worn to upscale and chic.

SOLUTION

- The soaring ceilings, wood paneling, and stone fireplace all contributed to the "lodge" feeling the couple loved, so I kept those elements but upgraded the look. Painting the walls at the back of the room, where the ceiling was dropped to single-story height, divided the space into zones, and painting the window trim really highlighted the windows as a feature.

- I designated the largest area, with the double-story ceiling, as the main seating area and the smaller part of the room, under the dropped ceiling, as the library/reading zone.

- To somewhat reduce the scale of the stone above the fireplace, I covered it with a huge framed mirror. It reflects the chandelier and views of the room and helps bounce light into the interior of the space.

- The five quirky windows let in a lot of natural light, but they are all different heights. To give them a more consistent look, I hung matching draperies at the same height over all of the windows, regardless of each window's height. That consistency plays them up as a feature and unifies them.

- Even with all of the windows, the room was dark because of the wood paneling on the walls and ceiling. To bring in more light, I added sconces, track lighting, and table lamps. I also replaced that huge wagon-wheel chandelier with a gorgeous, rustic, and elegant chandelier. It's centered over the seating and in front of the fireplace mirror for perfect reflection. I hung its baby-brother version in the library area. All of the lights are on dimmers, and since the control panel is at the top of the stairs, I included a cool little remote switch to save Fran and Jeff the hassle of running up and down the stairs every time they want to turn lights on or off, up or down.

OPPOSITE: The ceiling is so high that recessed lights wouldn't have made a dent in the light levels of the room, so I used track lights and a beautiful new chandelier to bring more illumination into the space. The huge mirror on the fireplace was so heavy it had to be hung on French cleats.

BELOW: The chandelier's little brother hangs in the library zone, where two cozy club chairs flank a round table. I painted the paneling in this area for a fresher look and brought in a mirror-fronted chest

STYLE ELEMENTS

- Since Fran and Jeff loved the big stone fireplace, I took that as the jumping-off point for colors, finishes, and furniture.

- With paneling the question is always "To paint or not to paint?" I opted to paint some of the walls sage green and all of the window trim crisp white to lighten and refresh the look without losing the rustic character the couple likes. Painting the paneling in the library area and the half-wall of the loft above it visually divides the room into zones and gives the library a more intimate feeling.

- To match the scale of the stone wall, I brought in large-scale furniture—two 9-foot, 6-inch sofas that are almost 4 feet deep. Now that's comfy! They're upholstered in sage-green brushed cotton for a casual feeling and centered on the fireplace to define the new lounge area.

- Behind one sofa in the lounge zone, I placed a small dining table and a pair of upholstered chairs. This area can be used for playing games or for casual meals.

- In the library/reading area, a pair of club chairs upholstered in antique leather brings in a more masculine feeling to balance all of the fabrics. Dark wood bookcases flank the windows.

- Lots of super-tall windows mean lots of fabric. I chose a linen-y tweed for the draperies and added a deep border of sage to speak to the sofa upholstery. Trimming the leading edge of each panel with a fabric that picks up the orange undertone in the stone and paneling brings all of the colors in the room together.

- For pattern and contrast, I accented the sofas with pillows in leafy-print, plaid, and starburst designs. The caramel and taupey tones are drawn from the stone, and the blues and greens speak to the views outdoors—the pool on one side and the canopy of trees on the other.

- To replace that "Westward ho!" wagon-wheel fixture, I chose a beautiful traditional chandelier with an antique finish. To hang at the right height for the room, it needs to drop nearly 6 feet from the ceiling! Its smaller companion chandelier hangs over the round table in the library area, giving that zone its own elegant, intimate feeling.

RIGHT: A big buffet provides much-needed storage. Its ebony finish, like that of the games table, brings in that touch of black or near-black that adds depth and weight to nearly any color scheme.

ABOVE: Furniture that's in scale with the space organizes the room into three clear zones: a games area, a lounging area, and a library/reading area. The beautiful wide-plank paneling and massive stone fireplace clearly say "lodge," while painted paneling at the library end of the room says "fresh and chic."

STYLE PLUS SUBSTANCE

CHALLENGE

Joanna and Al are young urban professionals who live in a modern, multi-level house with an open-concept layout that worked very well for the parties they used to host. But now the stork has landed, and late-night feedings have replaced the late-night parties. This super-hip couple has become super-safety conscious, and their home, especially the catwalks and open staircases, is definitely not baby-proof! They've asked me to solve the problem of creating a baby-friendly living room that is also urban-cool and comfy for entertaining grandparents.

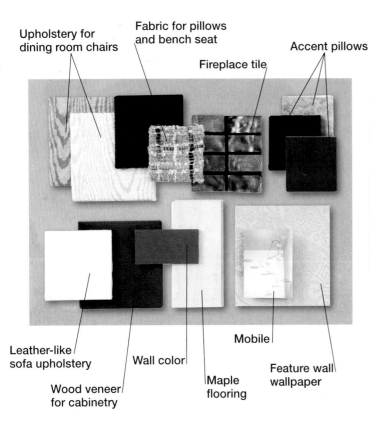

Upholstery for dining room chairs

Fabric for pillows and bench seat

Fireplace tile

Accent pillows

Leather-like sofa upholstery

Wood veneer for cabinetry

Wall color

Maple flooring

Mobile

Feature wall wallpaper

BEFORE: Industrial carpeting and a mishmash of hand-me-down furniture were fine for Joanna and Al's pre-parenthood parties, but the subterranean living–dining room didn't reflect their modern-but-not-stark sense of style at all. More important, the open staircase was a safety hazard for their new baby.

AFTER: Dramatic blocks of color give the new family space a contemporary, hip, downtown vibe. The white walls, ceiling, and bulkhead and the black cabinetry and mantel dance a visual tango with the black-and-white kitchen and help temper the impact of the bold color blocks.

SOLUTION

- The biggest safety issue was the staircase, which had open sides and risers. My remedy? Close up the stringers with MDF (medium-density fiberboard) attached to the underside of the staircase and paint it to blend in. I clad the railings with tempered-glass panels that preserve the feeling of openness while protecting baby Aaron from mishaps.

- The old industrial wall-to-wall carpeting made the basement-level living room feel like an office, so I ripped it up and laid down maple hardwood flooring. The flooring matches that in the rest of the house, and I installed it on top of subflooring specially designed for below-grade situations.

- The couple hated the old brick fireplace with its clunky, space-eating hearth. I tore out the hearth and removed the brick surround, then totally transformed the fireplace surround with a new cladding of tile. A new mantel and hearth custom-cut from shiny black quartz complete the facelift.

- I replaced the built-in open shelving beside the fireplace with wood-veneer cabinetry that lets the room multitask to accommodate baby and adults. Baby clutter can be stashed out of sight behind the closed doors, while the open shelves show off family photos.

- On the other side of the fireplace, I moved out the old free-standing cupboard and DVD tower and hung a flat-screen TV. I also continued the mantel across this space to serve as a display shelf.

- To pack more function into the sunken living room, I tucked a small home office under the stairs (see page 219) and added a dining area between the sitting area and the kitchen.

RIGHT: A gorgeous iridescent tile completely covers the old fireplace surround and provides the jumping-off point for the whole color scheme of fuchsia, teal, black, and white. New floor-to-ceiling cabinetry hides baby toys behind sleek black wood-veneer doors. The black quartz mantel continues across the fuchsia wall for more display space.

STYLE ELEMENTS

- Joanna and Al had recently redone the adjacent kitchen in black and white, so I continued that theme into the living room but kicked up the color quotient a notch—or two—with a fantastic peacock-inspired tile for the fireplace. The iridescent tiles shimmer with hues of black, purple, teal, gold, and fuchsia, making a gorgeous focal point for the room.

- I used the tile as the jumping-off point for big blocks of color that add drama to the space: fuchsia for two walls and a stunning teal-and-gold paisley wallpaper for a feature wall opposite the fireplace. To balance these bold colors, I painted everything else a clean, bright white.

- Joanna and Al need lots of comfy seating for visiting grandparents and friends. I brought in a long sectional and put one half against one wall and the other half against the feature wall. The matching bumper can be pushed up against the sofa to create a chaise or pulled away to open up more seating possibilities. These pieces are upholstered in a synthetic, leather-like fabric that's as soft as a baby's behind and cleans up with soap and water. So yes, you *can* have white upholstery with a baby!

- A low-arm chair and chaise covered in luscious, peacock-blue velvety upholstery round out the seating.

- To soften the corner where the chaise sits (and to visually continue the ceiling line around the atrium), I hung sheer, grommet-topped draperies at atrium level.

- The wall between the living area and the kitchen needed a big piece of art that could hold its own at eye level as well as from the floors above. I tried several before landing on a cool, contemporary abstract that brings in the teals, blues, and lime-greens of the fireplace tile.

- In the dining area, a new chic black table can shrink to seat two or expand to seat six when the extensions are added. Clean-lined dining chairs with cushiony upholstered backs and seats bring the room's white and teal colors over to the kitchen.

OPPOSITE: A spectacular laser-cut acrylic mirror is a shatterproof (thus baby-safe) way to expand space, reflect light, and call attention to the seating area. In front of the half-sectional, an upholstered bench also serves as a coffee table. Bold, saturated colors can be intimidating until you see them in context, with all of the furnishings and art in place.

BELOW: Above the chaise is a light well or atrium with a two-story window. I hung a Calder-like mobile in this space that should prove entertaining for both baby Aaron and Mom and Dad. Sheer draperies soften the corner and create a more continuous line at ceiling level for the sitting area.

BELOW: An abstract painting that picks up on the teal, blue, and green hues of the living room is a focal point not only for the dining room but also for the catwalks that overlook this space. Gleaming, natural-finish maple floors are clean and contemporary and relate to the flooring elsewhere in the house.

ABOVE: A beautiful teal-and-gold paisley wallpaper sets off the other half of the sectional. Combined with a big, cushy bumper, the sofa becomes a chaise. The accent pillows add contrasting pattern and pick up all of the colors: black, fuchsia, and teal.

RIGHT: I baby-proofed the stairs with panels of tempered glass attached to the railings and enclosed the stairs with MDF underneath. Painted white, the MDF blends with the railings, walls, and ceiling.

OPPOSITE: A simple black desk topped with glass and a compact desk chair turn the under-stairs nook into a home office.

INDEX